T0222860

Voice User Interface Design

Moving from GUI to Mixed Modal Interaction

Ritwik Dasgupta

Apress®

Voice User Interface Design: Moving from GUI to Mixed Modal Interaction

Ritwik Dasgupta
Hyderabad, Telangana, India

ISBN-13 (pbk): 978-1-4842-4124-0   ISBN-13 (electronic): 978-1-4842-4125-7
https://doi.org/10.1007/978-1-4842-4125-7

Library of Congress Control Number: 2018966797

Copyright © 2018 by Ritwik Dasgupta

Managing Director, Apress Media LLC: Welmoed Spahr
Acquisitions Editor: Smriti Srivastava
Development Editor: Laura Berendson
Coordinating Editor: Shrikant Vishwakarma

Cover designed by eStudioCalamar

Cover image designed by Freepik (www.freepik.com)

Distributed to the book trade worldwide by Springer Science+Business Media New York, 233 Spring Street, 6th Floor, New York, NY 10013. Phone 1-800-SPRINGER, fax (201) 348-4505, e-mail orders-ny@springer-sbm.com, or visit www.springeronline.com. Apress Media, LLC is a California LLC and the sole member (owner) is Springer Science + Business Media Finance Inc (SSBM Finance Inc). SSBM Finance Inc is a **Delaware** corporation.

For information on translations, please e-mail rights@apress.com, or visit http://www.apress.com/rights-permissions.

Apress titles may be purchased in bulk for academic, corporate, or promotional use. eBook versions and licenses are also available for most titles. For more information, reference our Print and eBook Bulk Sales web page at http://www.apress.com/bulk-sales.

Any source code or other supplementary material referenced by the author in this book is available to readers on GitHub via the book's product page, located at www.apress.com/978-1-4842-4124-0. For more detailed information, please visit http://www.apress.com/source-code.

Printed on acid-free paper

Table of Contents

About the Author vii

About the Contributor ix

About the Technical Reviewers xi

Chapter 1: Introduction to VUI 1

    When Did It All Start? 2

    Era of Digital Assistants 3

    Why Use Voice? 6

    The Current Landscape 8

    Moving Forward 11

Chapter 2: Principles of VUI 13

    Recognize Intent 15

        Example 1 16

        Analysis 18

        Example 2 18

        Analysis 18

        Example 3 19

        Analysis 20

    Leverage Context 21

        Example 1 22

        Analysis 23

        Example 2 23

Analysis 23

Example 3 24

Analysis 24

Cooperate and Respond 26

Progressive Disclosure 31

Variety 34

Give and Take 35

Moving Forward 37

Chapter 3: Personality **39**

Why Do We Need to Create a Personality? 42

Users Know That They Are Talking to a Voice Assistant Who Helps
Get Things Done 43

Users Know That They Are Talking to a Voice Assistant When They
Are Also Interacting with a Screen (Multi-Modal) 44

Users Do Not Know That They Are Talking to a Voice Assistant 50

Using Hesitation Markers 55

Adding Pauses 56

Moving Forward 66

Chapter 4: The Power of Multi-Modal Interactions **67**

What Is User Interface Design (UI) and User Experience (UX) Design? 71

User Experience Design (UX) 73

Usability and Types of Interactions 75

Unimodal Graphical User Interface Systems (GUI Systems) 77

Graphical User Interfaces (GUI)/WIMP Interactions 78

Voice Interactions 78

Gestural Interfaces 80

Haptics 81

Multi-Modal Interactions 82

Unimodal Graphical User Interface Systems (GUI Systems) vs Multi-Modal
Interfaces 86

Principles of User Interactions 89

    Visibility of System Status 91

    Flexibility of System Status 92

    Aesthetic and Minimalist Design 93

Emerging Multi-Modal Principles 95

Designing the Voice-Based Interface 96

Summary 103

Index 105

About the Author

Ritwik Dasgupta works as a UX designer with Microsoft, India. He works on the Cortana team for Windows 10, assistant-enabled devices, and iOS and Android apps. He received his Bachelor's of Architecture degree from NIT Calicut and his postgraduate degree in Industrial Design (MDes) from IIT Delhi.

About the Contributor

 **Akshat Verma** completed his masters in new media design from the National Institute of Design. He has actively worked on voice user interfaces, interaction design, Voice UX, context-aware computing, user interface design, and experience design using technologies to create new and engaging experiences on screens and beyond.

He is currently working in AVP Innovation Design & Technology at the Newzstreet Media Group and looks after product development and identifying potential strategies for fulfilling business revenue opportunities with the product updates and features.

He has specialized his focus area on voice-based UI systems to create new experiences, having already worked to create successful voice interactions on Amazon Alexa and Google Home technologies in the Indian markets.

He previously worked with the global strategy team at Honeywell (HTS) on voice recognition technology while exploring the areas of context-aware computing and was part of the core team that designed India's first audio e-learning platform called I-Radiolive.com.

About the Technical Reviewers

Simonie Wilson has worked in speech and voice user interfaces for 20+ years. Her career in Computational Linguistics has taken her from big companies like Microsoft and GM to startups, contracting, and back again. With a masters from Georgetown University, Simonie has participated in numerous conferences and workshops and holds a patent in dialog design. Her current focus is on usability and best practices for these systems and the tools used to build and tune them.

Kasam Shaikh is a certified Azure architect, global AI speaker, technical blogger, and C# Corner MVP. He has more than 10 years of experience in the IT industry and is a regular speaker at various events on Azure. He is also a founder of DearAzure.net. He leads the Azure India (azINDIA) online community, the fastest growing online community for learning Microsoft Azure. He has a concrete technical background with good hands-on experience in Microsoft technologies. At DearAzure.net, he has been organizing online free webinars and live events for learning Microsoft Azure. He also gives sessions and speaks on developing bots with Microsoft Azure cognitive and QnA Maker service at international conferences, online communities, and local user groups. He owns a YouTube channel and shares his experience over his web site at https://www.kasamshaikh.com.

CHAPTER 1

Introduction to VUI

This is 2019. The year becomes significant when we start talking technological advancements and their effects as we move forward. Every year, we see something new, something that has the potential to change technology forever. But as American fiction author William Gibson puts it aptly, "The future is already here; it is just not very evenly distributed." The year acts as a milestone, a benchmark for the immense amount of effort for the entire civilization to reach to this point, and shows where we are headed in the near future.

Voice User Interface (or VUI) is an interaction model where a human interacts with a machine and performs a set of tasks at least in part by using voice. For example, "Hey Siri, tell me today's headlines" is a simple VUI command where Siri identifies and "tells" the user the news as output. In a similar manner, IVR (Interactive Voice Response) systems are widely used in the banking and travel industries. These systems are primarily dependent on voice biometrics for identifying the users and choosing the set of tasks that the user wants to complete using voice as a primary interaction mode.

The explosion of VUI has come about at the same time that major companies have started experimenting with fluid cross-device experiences. We live in a time where Alexa aims to become our go-to shopping assistant, Google is our search assistant, and Cortana is our work assistant. Imagine using an travel booking web site to book a flight. Once the flight booking is completed and the travel details are confirmed, the

© Ritwik Dasgupta 2018
R. Dasgupta, *Voice User Interface Design*, https://doi.org/10.1007/978-1-4842-4125-7_1

various assistants set automated reminders on your phone to remind you to catch your flight or to show you the traffic conditions before catching your flight so that you may reach the airport on time.

But voice recognition is not a new technology.

When Did It All Start?

An experimental device designed by IBM in 1961, the *Shoebox* was an early effort at mastering voice recognition. The machine recognized 16 words spoken into its microphone and converted those sounds into electrical impulses. It was first demonstrated at the 1962 World's Fair in Seattle by its developer, William C. Dersch of the Advanced Systems Development division. The name given was *Shoebox,* owing to its small size. This was the beginning of two new technologies—Automated Speech Recognition (ASR) and Natural Language Understanding (NLU). This dealt with only the first part—voice recognition. For a pure voice-user interface, the machine needed to generate a human voice. This was experimented on even earlier, as early as 1939.

The Voder by Homer Dudley (Bell Telephone Laboratories, Murray Hill, New Jersey) was the first device that could generate continuous human speech electronically. In 1939, Alden P. Armagnac wrote in *Popular Science* magazine about this speaking device. It was created from vacuum tubes and electrical circuits, by Bell Telephone Laboratories engineers. It was meant to duplicate the human voice. To manufacture conversation, the machine operator employed a keyboard like that of an organ. Thirteen black and white keys produced all the vowels and consonants of speech. Another key regulated the loudness of the synthetic voice, which came from a loudspeaker. A foot pedal varied the inflection so that the same sentence may state a fact or ask a question. About a year's practice enabled an operator to make the machine speak.

Time magazine wrote on January 16th, 1939, that Bell Telephone demonstrators made it clear that Voder did not reproduce speech, like a telephone receiver or loudspeaker. It created speech via an operator who synthesized sounds to form words. Twenty-three basic sounds were created by a skilled operator using a keyboard and foot pedal. Two dozen operators trained for a year.

The VUIs were interactive voice response (IVR) systems that understood human speech over the telephone in order to carry out tasks. In the early 2000s, IVR systems became mainstream. Anyone with a phone could book plane flights, transfer money between accounts, order prescription refills, find local movie times, and hear traffic information, all using nothing more than a regular phone and the human voice.

So, how does this put "today's" technology into perspective?

Technologies like voice interaction, augmented reality, and virtual reality, among others have been present or been researched for a relatively long time. What makes the current offerings exciting is that they are finally widely commercially available, and we have a need for designers and engineers who can take up the challenge to develop scenarios to solve everyday problems for the user.

This is very similar to when GUI became the norm for human-machine interaction, where we felt the need for designers to clear up the clutter, simplify the data, and present the users with flows and solutions that were easier to grasp. Let's take a TV remote as an example. It can be extremely difficult to operate one when we have 20-30 buttons on the device and it becomes difficult for a person to comprehend what all the buttons do. Without good design, technology is difficult or even impossible to use.

We need to realize that we are in the next era of VUIs—the era of digital assistants. At present, there are many things that a digital assistant can do well by voice, but there are still many things it just cannot do.

Era of Digital Assistants

We are gradually getting more and more dependent on digital assistants like Siri and Alexa to get information or do tasks. But there are two types of assistants—one that uses only text to interact with us, which includes chatbots like Ruuh—and the other that uses multiple modes of interaction like voice and GUI to interact with us, such as Alexa and Google assistant.

Chatbots are generally much easier to build as compared to more complicated AI bots and they also require less infrastructure. They are mainly focused on a single purpose—for example to cha—and to provide very linear and single dimensional support—for example, customer service. A chatbot is an interactive virtual agent or artificial conversation entity that conducts a conversation with a user within the context that it is implemented. An example of this type of agent is how a DTH company implements a chatbot-based system on their web site, rather than implementing a dedicated customer support agent. The chatbot can easily troubleshoot basic support issues, such as recharging or resetting user accounts when they are not working.

A chatbot can be built with numerous goals in mind:

- eCommerce support either directly, like like CentlyBot, or as an influencer, like KalaniBot.

- Some can be for pure conversational entertainment, like Mitsuku, Xiaoice, and Humani.

- Others can have assistant-like goals, such as Hipmunk, Growbot, or Howdy.

- They can even fall in between, like Poncho, which tries to bring amusement in addition to reporting the weather.

Digital assistants, on the other hand, have been made specifically to perform simple to complex tasks for the user, instead of carefully creating and continuing a conversation. This separation is important. For example, you want your digital assistant to search for a good Italian restaurant and book a table for two. A digital assistant like Siri or Alexa will show you the search results and then proceed to book your table.

A chatbot (see Figure 1-1) that's built for the sole purpose of chatting, on the other hand, will digress and the conversation will move to more generic topics like weather, traffic, and who you are going out with. When a task needs to be accomplished, seeming more human can actually be a hindrance. The chatbot systems are based on AI and are built for specific use cases, and for each of these cases, the chatbots seem to act like a normal human by design. Unfortunately, the moment the system is exposed to a novel use case, the system will seemingly fail to solve the user's request. It is therefore best to showcase the system as artificial for the user to be able to interact with it, recognizing in fact that it isn't human.

Figure 1-1. Example of a conversation by a chatbot named Mitsuku. Source: Akiwatkar, Rohit; "What are the best and most intelligent chatbots in the market right now?", Quora, April 20, 2017.

Why Use Voice?

Using voice as a means of interaction has distinct advantages over chatbots and digital assistants:

- **Intuitive**—Using voice to interact is the most natural form of interaction. GUI, or interacting with a screen, is a learned behavior, and it's unnatural in some sense. Infants, even when they learn to interact with screens, are inept or have difficulty when the interaction patterns differ from app to app. However, voice interaction with another person, its modality, principles, and patterns, remain universal. A person learns to talk once, but he/she has to learn to use a new app/device each time.

- **Hands free**—This is an advantage that dictates a scenario like driving, cooking, etc. The scenario dictates the mode of interaction.

- **Speed**—Taking a note by using a recorder, instead of typing it, is always faster. But processing a voice command and generating a reply is a whole different issue. Still, by way of design, it takes immensely less time to perform a task by voice.

  Suppose you have to set a reminder for watering the plants at 7AM every morning. If we use GUI to perform this task, we need to provide certain data sets like "watering the plants," "7AM," and "everyday," which is essentially three-four mouse clicks minimum. Also, we generally use a native Android or iOS timepicker to set the time.

Imagine the same scenario with a smart speaker. All we need to say is "Remind me to water the plants every day at 7AM". This single command does all these things at a single go, making this mode of interaction immensely faster.

- **Personas**—All users tend to associate a personality with a device or machine even when it doesn't have one due to the way it is designed. This is one reason an iPhone looks "cool". This comes down to product design and how a designer has given certain qualities to a product through his design. This becomes evident when we look at cars; we can associate distinct personality types with different brands of cars.

We build relationships with other humans through emotional connection rather than just mere information exchange. We act and remain attached, not because of reason, but because of emotions we display. We eventually become attached. Clearly a digital assistant's personality must be consistent across scenarios and channels. But on top of that, it must also forge an emotional bond with its users and adjust to their personalities and to the circumstances of the interaction.

Linguistic alignment is the tendency of humans to mimic their conversational partner. This is an important consideration when designing virtual assistants as well.

We will delve deeper whether a personality is needed or not and the implications of this issue in the coming chapters.

The Current Landscape

This section presents my personal opinions regarding the current landscape in VUI. This segment has four major players right now—Apple, Google, Amazon, and Microsoft. Each are targeting a specific market segment with a specific intent, which aligns with their company's visions and goals.

Apple has made a bet on personality with Siri, but the service lacks the features of a more robust digital assistant (for example, it's missing personalization and understanding context over time). Google is focusing on using contextual awareness and search history to deliver proactive experiences through Google Now; however, it lacks thoughtful cohesiveness and the delight of a more personal digital assistant. There is some habituation around a small set of tasks, but neither competitor has developed a service with a strong daily presence that users cannot live without. Today's digital assistants from most of the companies—such as Apple (Siri), Amazon (Alexa), Google Now, and Microsoft Cortana—have made serious improvements in leaps and bounds to make the interactions much more joyful and fun, but they are yet to fully utilize the complete functionality that could help them become smart assistants in the future in our homes/offices and other relevant surroundings.

Google has divided the digital assistant landscape into three major parts—Google Now, Google Assistant/Allo, and Google Home. Google Now takes care of content based on your search history and interests; Allo works both as a standard chat app and an assistant app using conversational user interface with voice assistance, and Google Home integrates all the connected devices together.

Google, as of now, aims to create a private, personalized Internet for you, whereby what you see is what you wish to see. This does have an inherent bias as it does not offer the full impartial multiple faces of the Internet. It is catered specifically to you and your tastes.

Google has started investing heavily in hardware to facilitate its vision, as it recently released Pixel 2, the AI-powered Clips camera, Home mini, and a few more. Google has also heavily invested in AI, and the way they have been implementing it is pretty clear—they care less about being Google Assistant and care more about being present everywhere.

As the first digital assistant to hit the market and the one of the most widely publicized, Apple's Siri continues to be relevant to our competitor conversation since its debut in 2010. That said, Siri has yet to make any serious play in the realms of context or personalization. While Siri made the first industry attempt at a digital assistant with personality, it's a very superficial treatment. Upon last inspection, the system makes no attempt to get to know its users, nor to tailor the experience over time to be better suited to their needs.

Siri's personality consists largely of a set of rotating quips and witty responses in cases when the system doesn't know an answer, or simple ways like referring to the user by name.

But this year Apple has released its much awaited HomePod speaker, which also has its own set of limitations.

I don't think I've ever described a tech product as "lonely" before, but it's the word I thought about the most as I was reviewing Apple's new HomePod. This is simply because it demands that you live entirely inside Apple's ecosystem in a way that even Apple's other products do not. Also, it has way fewer number of skills compared to Alexa or Google as of this writing. This means it can perform fewer tasks compared to other assistants. This seems to be a bane for Apple as it would not run in the rat race for more skills, so it will go specifically for quality. This is similar to the Apple App Store versus Android Play Store race. But, as of now, just to get better access to the newly formed market, companies have strived to make numbers.

Verge, a well known Internet technology magazine, has an interesting take on HomePod. According to *Verge*[1], "when Apple researched what most people ask their smart speakers for, it found that playing music the most popular use, asking for the weather is second, and setting timers and

---

[1]Patel, Nilay; "Apple HomePod Review: Locked In," *The Verge,* Feb 6, 2018, https://www.theverge.com/2018/2/6/16976906/apple-homepod-review-smart-speaker.

reminders is third. So, it's baffling that the HomePod can't set more than one timer or name those timers; anyone who cooks with a smart speaker in their kitchen knows how incredibly useful that is. You can't ask Siri to look up a recipe. You can't ask Siri to make a phone call. (You have to start the phone call on your phone and transfer it to the HomePod to use it as a just-okay speakerphone.) Siri also can't compete with the huge array of Amazon Alexa skills, or Google Assistant's ability to answer a vast variety of questions."

Alexa is your almost perfect shopping assistant, at least for now. Integrating Amazon Prime for shopping, videos, and now, music has given users a very easy choice to buy into the Amazon ecosystem. Amazon has been specifically going for quantity rather than quality. They have been consistently targeting holiday season sales by bringing in a plethora of products with Alexa built-in. They have also kept their price range to a minimum, making it an easier gifting option too. Their mantra is simply "Alexa everywhere".

This is beautifully put by Larry Dignan at znet.com,[2] "On the strategy front, Amazon's strategy with Alexa rhymes with what we've seen from Netflix and Microsoft in the past. Netflix dropped allegiance to hardware and partnered with multiple vendors to distribute its service. Microsoft's Windows operating system wasn't the best game in town in the early days of the PC market but gained distribution to become a standard."

---

[2]Dignan, Larry; "At CES 2017, Amazon revs Alexa everywhere strategy," *Between the Lines,* znet.com, January 3, 2017.

Moving Forward

As we move forward, we will be talking about different use cases and their problems for specific digital assistants in the market. There are various limitations, both in technology and design for voice versus GUI.

As it turns out, comprehending language is not exactly easy. It's filled with subtleties and idiosyncrasies that take humans years to develop. Decades were spent trying to program computers to understand the simplest of commands. It was believed by some that only an entity who lived in the physical world could ever truly understand language, because it needs to understand the meanings of words in different contexts. These are challenges that are extremely relevant today.

CHAPTER 2

Principles of VUI

"Speech is the fundamental means of human communication. Even when other forms of communication—such as writing, facial expressions, or sign language—would be equally expressive, (hearing people) in all cultures to persuade, inform, and build relationships primarily through speech."

—Clifford Nass and Scott Brave,
Stanford researchers and authors[1]

As we saw in Chapter 1, the journey has been long, and we are still in the nascent stages of this evolution in our technology. In this chapter we will discuss the principles of VUI and specific use cases to show you how to create good designs.

Voice User Interface (VUI) design is dependent on conversation. In the book on voice interaction, *Wired for Speech,* Stanford researchers Clifford Nass and Scott Brave argue that users to some extent relate to voice interfaces in the same way that they relate to other people. Since speech/conversation is so fundamental to human communication, we cannot completely disregard our expectations for how normal human-to-human speech communication takes place, even if we are fully aware that we are speaking to a device rather than a person.

---

[1]Nass, Clifford, Brave, Scott; *Wired for Speech: How Voice Activates and Advances the Human-Computer Relationship,* MIT Press, 2007.

© Ritwik Dasgupta 2018
R. Dasgupta, *Voice User Interface Design*, https://doi.org/10.1007/978-1-4842-4125-7_2

Conversation is a complex but systematic medium, with principles that are subtle and compelling. When we interact with other humans, we take the complexity of conversation in stride; it's already second nature. But when we are designing spoken dialogue with a device, not understanding the true, inner workings of conversation will result in a negative experience. And because voice is a personal marker of an individual's identity, the stakes are high—users of poorly designed VUIs report feeling "foolish," "silly," and manipulated by technology, and so they avoid repeat usage.

Conversation design is a powerful approach, but it may not be right for every scenario. For example, conversation works well for finding the nearest movie theater, but it feels clunky for browsing a dinner menu. Before you decide to use conversation, evaluate whether it will help ease your scenario's pain points, making it more intuitive and efficient for users.

Before designing a conversation, we need to be mindful of whether it fulfills the following criteria:

1. The interaction is generally short, with minimum back and forth interactions.

2. Users can do this task through conversation even though they are busy and cannot pay full attention.

3. User feels a lot of lag or pain while doing the same task through GUI and conversation will help ease the pain.

Let's take an example:

"Are there any Italian restaurants nearby?"

We need to check whether this scenario satisfies the stated criteria.

- ✓ Users generally have voice conversations with each other regarding a particular task in hand.

- ✓ The interaction is generally short, with minimum back and forth interactions.

- ✓ Users can do this task through conversation even though they are busy and cannot pay full attention.

- ✓ Users feel a lot of lag or pain while doing the same task through GUI and conversation will help ease the pain.

In this scenario, conversation is better because it is intuitive to use, saves the user time and effort, allows for multitasking, and is just easier than opening a browser, typing, waiting for search results, and then reading them.

For designing simple and effective conversations, I will detail some principles that we need to be mindful of.

Recognize Intent

The intent can be defined as the objective of a user's voice command, and this can either be a low-utility or high-utility interaction.

A high-utility interaction is about performing a very specific task, such as requesting that the AC in the bedroom be turned off. Designing for these requests is easy since it's very clear what's expected from the assistant.

Low-utility requests are more vague and harder to decipher. For example, if a user wants to buy a laptop, it is hard to understand the specifications or criteria that matter to him/her personally that will motivate the act of buying. Then it becomes harder for us to design without knowing the user's personal choices.

When designing for GUI, designers think about what information is more important/primary, and what information is secondary. Users do not want to feel overloaded, but they need enough information to complete the task.

When designing for voice, designers have to be even more careful because words (and maybe a relatively simple GUI) are all that there is to communicate with. This makes it all the more difficult in the case of conveying complex information. This means we need to keep the conversation short and effective, no matter what. If we are having a lengthy conversation, that will be under the purview of chitchat and not for completing any task.

Before we dive further into the principles, there is one more thing that needs to be kept in mind. We need to avoid assuming that people will say precisely the words that you anticipate for an intent. While the user might say "search for restaurants nearby," he or she could just as easily say "show me a restaurant nearby." To make sure the interaction is successful, we need to provide a wide range of sentences, phrases, and words that people are likely to say to call for the specific intent. A good benchmark is 30 or more utterances per intent, even for simple intents. You do not need 100% coverage, but the more examples, the better it is. Also, plan to continue adding utterances over time to improve performance after analyzing usage data.

Example 1

I will call my voice assistant, Max. Let's see an example:

> *Me: I am really hungry.*

> *Max: Have you been to the Fisherman's Wharf?*

This is an extremely simple example to show the underlying complexity in voice design. This conversation sounds exactly like one between humans, but we do not realize the layer of thoughts we put into before uttering a word. In this example, Max is actually responding in an intelligent way. The response has certain assumptions in place:

1. Fisherman's Wharf serves food.

2. I like seafood.

3. It is open for business at this very moment.

4. It is probably nearby or at a driving distance.

5. I have not been to this place yet.

Let's look at each assumption:

1. Max knows the list of places that serve food.

2. Max knows my interests in food.

3. Max knows when a particular restaurant is open.

4. Max knows whether I have a car, prefer driving, and my average distance of travel.

5. Max knows that I have not been to this place, or else he would have said "Do you want to go to your favorite restaurant, the Fisherman's Wharf?"

Conversation is rarely literal; we have to understand the user's intentions by drawing inferences from hundreds of conversations. Let's imagine this same conversation in a more literal way

> *Me: I am really hungry.*
>
> *Max: You can cook something, order food, or go to a restaurant. Which one do you prefer?*
>
> *Me: I would prefer to go to a restaurant.*
>
> *Max: Which cuisine do you prefer?*
>
> *Me: Seafood*
>
> *Max: There are five seafood restaurants nearby—a, b, c, d, and Fisherman's Wharf. Which one do you prefer?*
>
> *Me: Fisherman's Wharf*

Analysis

The same conversation turned into a long and elaborate conversation by trying to detail out each module along the way. This made the conversation verbose. This type of conversation looks exactly how a customer care conversation looks, doesn't it? Would you want to talk to this person multiple times a day? Would you employ this person to take care of your business? Maybe not.

Instead, we need to build a conversation that seems natural, understands the user's intent, and responds intelligently.

Example 2

> *Me: Max, I am tired.*
>
> *Max: I am sorry, I did not understand.*

It seems Max does not know my intent. Let's assume Max has access to my calendar, in which case Max can understand the intent and offer more.

> *Me: Max, I am tired.*
>
> *Max: I understand. You have had a long day full of meetings. Want to watch Netflix?*

Analysis

Max realized that "tiredness" is connected to the activity that I have been doing and whether that activity is something that is part of my usual day, which is important here. Max realizes that I have been busier than usual. After understanding the intent, Max could have easily just said "I understand; you have had a long day full of meetings" but Max understood the intent and offered a suggestion.

Example 3

> *Me: Max, winter is coming.*

This is quite vague, right? What should I do with this piece of information? Do I want Max to set a reminder for winter? Do I want Max to plan my Christmas? What is the intent here?

Humans typically know what the intent is due to our "shared world information". We know that the user is referring to a *Game of Thrones* quote and wants a response that is more context dependent. This is how Max would respond if he does not know my intent:

> *Me: Max, winter is coming.*

> *Max: Yes, winter will begin on Saturday, 22*
> *December. Do you want me to set a reminder for that?*

Max has recognized the intent and offered more. But it doesn't seem appropriate. People imply things without saying them out loud.

Figure 2-1 shows how Google Assistant responds to the same query.

Figure 2-1. *Google response to a query*

Funny, right? Wasn't that the intent when I asked about winter? A simple line might have an entirely different meaning when you recognize the intent with which it is said. As we move forward, we see that "shared world knowledge" becomes an important construct to recognize intent.

Analysis

What is shared world knowledge? It becomes the entirety of world data, including types and patterns of speech that we use in our daily life. An alien will not understand if I said, "It's raining cats and dogs here". What will the alien think? You might find the same problem happening when you visit a foreign country. It is difficult to know what the other person is implying with his/her mannerisms and body language. In some places, clapping your hands after a performance means that you admired and enjoyed it; in another culture, being completely silent after the performance mean the same. For example, when a boxer from the United States fought Buster Douglas in Tokyo, the fight was full of action and entertainment, but there was complete silence all around during the bout. The corner men who were from United States were confused because a similar bout in America would have dramatically increased the decibel levels in the stadium.

Shared world knowledge is therefore local and global at the same time. Voice assistants need to understand this. If an Indian and an American ask Max separately, "When is the next football match?", the intent is entirely different. The American is most probably looking for an American football match, whereas the Indian is wondering about soccer matches.

Leverage Context

In her book, *Plans and Situated Actions: The Problem of Human-Machine Communication,* Lucy Suchman[2] describes human communication as situated and context bound. The data is not naturally contained in just the spoken aspect of the message when people have a conversation. Humans use knowledge of the context to create shared meaning as they listen and talk.

For a voice recognition technology, grasping all the contextual factors and assumptions in a brief exchange is almost impossible. Until the state of the art changes to the point that it can stretch to accommodate idiomatic expressions, we will need to make users understand the need for keeping their phraseology direct and basic. That way, the voice engines won't be thrown by ambiguity or what they might register as indecipherable signals. We also need to remember that English is a very quirky language, often having four or five words for the same entity, whereas other languages have, at best two. This can create more confusion in case it fails to recognize the context.

Next time you sit down for a dinner conversation with friends, try to understand where and when you and your friends switch context. There are numerous times we do it unconsciously and there are times when we have difficulty understanding context as well. The conversation may start with the weather, then switch to the traffic, after which one of your friends begins telling a story of how they got stuck in traffic and missed a flight and so on. Try to imagine each piece of conversation as a frame. This frame can be based on topic of discussion, time, location, the person who is speaking, or the emotion represented. Then try to imagine how difficult it would be for a voice assistant to keep track of these same switches.

---

[2]Suchman, Lucy; *Plans and Situated Actions: The Problem of Human-Machine Communication,* Cambridge University Press, 1987.

How can emotion be a frame? As someone talks about how they felt when they missed their flight, I understand the emotion from my perspective and I share a story of how I felt when I missed my job interview due to traffic. I connect to my friend's topic through my own experiences, but the connecting chain here is the emotion involved.

If the frames are captured sequentially, understood, and saved, it represents a context chain for an assistant. Similarly, humans unconsciously map the memory to store a conversation.

Suppose you are chatting with your friend Susan about the weather, then traffic, then a flight delay, and so on. In the midst of this conversation, you get a phone call from your manager about some issue. You hang up the phone but by then, both of you have forgotten the context of the ongoing conversation. What do you do then? You can trace your conversation from past to present, each frame as a conversation, to try to understand the context of the present one. This happens multiple times in our daily lives and we hardly ever notice it.

Let's look at examples where voice assistants need to understand context and respond accordingly.

Example 1

> Me: Max, what is the height of Mt. Everest?
>
> Max: Mt. Everest is 8,848 meters high.
>
> Me: Which one is the second highest?

At this point, Max needs to understand that I am still taking about mountains and I want to know the second tallest mountain. We humans do this every day all the time. For example, I had this conversation with a friend.

> Me: What is the height of Mt. Everest?
>
> Friend: I think it's 8,000 something meters high.
>
> Me: We could go for a trek.

Friend: Get some food. You need to eat so that you make some sense.

Me: Which one is the second highest?

Friend: I think it's K2.

Analysis

My friend understood the context even when the conversation was diverted to a trek, food, and what-not. He understood that I was still talking about mountain peaks. Understanding context is vital for a voice assistant because humans take this principle for granted while conversing and the lack of it results in frustration.

Simple context recognition is still difficult for assistants. Take this example.

Example 2

Me: What is the weather outside?

Max: Its 16C outside, with heavy showers

Me: How long will it take to drive to the office ?

Max: Driving to office will take around 20 minutes in the current weather conditions. You should leave early to get to your meeting at noon.

Analysis

This small change in timing and understanding that there is a meeting to reach on time creates a feeling of trust and surprise. Understanding context regularly and responding accordingly will make users trust your assistant because of the personality attributed to him. This trust is slowly earned through the personality, which allows users to become at ease and to converse with the assistant. They will happily come back time and again.

Example 3

Understanding context also helps in other scenarios. Suppose the assistant added a new fitness ability, where it can track users' morning runs. How do you upsell this to your potential users? When exactly during the day should you inform the users about this? Do you inform the users when they are in the office, or when they are at the gym? Do you tell them in the morning or at night? These decisions are crucial to the success of the assistant.

Analysis

Suppose Piper's daily routine involves asking Max about her meetings in the morning, then going for a run, then going to the office and coming back around four, going to the gym, spending some time with her family, planning her next day, and going to sleep.

Here, I see three potential areas/time instances for upselling a fitness ability.

- When Piper wakes up and asks Max about her day, Max can reply with "Good morning; it's a nice day today with no showers and a high of 25C. Your first meeting today is at 11:30. By the way, I have a new ability just for you. Now I can track your morning runs. Interested?"

- Just after the run, Piper takes out her phone and there is a notification saying, "Want to track your morning runs?"

- After her gym, when she is in the cab, Piper gets notified about the new fitness ability.

Understanding context helps in three ways:

- **Physical context**—Where is the person and what is she doing?

- **Emotional context**—Just returning after jogging, what is her mental state? Is there any problem area that you can solve at the right moment?

- **Conversational context**—What was she just talking about? Are we still talking about the same thing or has the conversation shifted?

Response after understanding context is important too. I said I was tired. Max understood the context that it was because of my multiple meetings throughout the day. Max understood and empathized with me. Emotional context is vital for creating a habit and a support system.

Suppose I query "Ways to commit suicide" in Google. It should show me ways to commit suicide, because that's what a search engine is supposed to do. Instead, it shows the result in Figure 2-2.

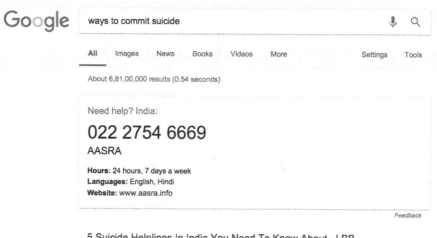

Figure 2-2. *Google understands the emotional context of a difficult query*

Google understands the emotional context beautifully here and responds accordingly. Sometimes, we have to go out of our way to respond accordingly. At the end of the day, the voice assistants are not conversing with machines, but humans, and humans are not independent from their emotions. They are always under their influence. We need to recognize and respect that even when designing assistants.

From physical, emotional, and conversational context, we can create an inference or reach a conclusion about what the conversation is about. These inferences are mapped through time and we get to know the user more and more over time, including their habits, interests, preferences, and more.

Cooperate and Respond

Humans are social animals and we socialize mainly through speech. We have a clear demarcation between people we know and strangers. This is due to the number/length of conversations we have had together, the number of mutual friends, shared interests, and the level of trust between the two individuals.

The same is applicable to voice assistants. We tend to give a face to a person or object even if they have none. This is called *anthropomorphizing*. Humans tend to anthropomorphize every object we see, living or non-living. Not only that, but we may try to interact with the object very similarly to how we talk to other humans. We want to know more about the object/individual, such as our shared choices and interests, in order to develop a sense of trust so that we build a relationship and even a habit of conversing.

For voice assistants, there can be two types of conversations:

- Intent-based conversations

- Casual conversations

Intent-based conversations are the ones we have in order to fulfill an objective or complete a task. We have an intent in mind and we want answers from the assistant. We simply want to complete a task.

Casual conversations are where users are interacting with the assistant without a specific intent. They just want to talk to the assistant, talk about interests, perhaps to learn more about each other and build a relationship.

There are different types of chatbots based exactly on this difference. But as we move forward, and our natural language capabilities become better, we have more confidence in building assistants that can behave more like a human and not disappoint its users. This results in a mixed approach, where every conversation can be delightful and we get to know more about the objective or about the assistant.

Let's look at this example first:

> Me: Do you know who is playing in the World Cup
> tomorrow?
>
> Max: Yes.
>
> Me: Can you order from Domino's?
>
> Max: No

In these two short examples, we see that the assistant is responding correctly to each question. They were supposed to answer yes/no. But does it sound cooperative in both cases? Does it sound inviting? No. This brings us back to the first principle of intent.

There are three ways to respond to fully satisfy a question:

1. If the question is vague, ask for more details.

2. If the answer is No, suggest an alternative or show a way to satisfy the said intent.

3. Give more than what was expected. This does not mean that the assistant blurts out every bit of information that it has on the topic. I cover "progressive disclosure" in the coming pages.

27

Let's take examples for each response.

> *Me: Do you know who is playing in the World Cup tomorrow?*
>
> *Max: We have the semifinal coming up, where England is playing Croatia in the World Cup tomorrow.*

Max gave one extra bit of information about it being the semifinal.

> *Me: Can you order from Domino's?*
>
> *Max: Domino's isn't supported in this region, but you can order from Pizza Hut if you like. Are you interested?*

Max gives an alternative, as the answer is no. Humans want assistants to assist; humans aren't there to assist the assistant. So, it's the job of the assistant to understand what was said and find an answer.

Let's take another example.

> *Me: Max, what can you do for me?*
>
> *Max: I can set alarms for you. Just say "Max, set an alarm for 7AM". For more options, say "Tell me more".*

This just sounds unnatural. Humans do not talk like that. Think how an assistant would have responded.

> *Me: Max, what can you do for me?*
>
> *Max: I can set alarms for you. I can also set reminders for you. Do you want to hear some more things I can do?*

This sounds more natural, as you expect the user to know how to set an alarm. Max doesn't respond like a call center executive where one responds, "For a, press 1, for b, press 2". Instead, Max leverages the art of human conversation. Giving conditions like these for a response is a threat to conversations where it seems like you have to press a particular button to open new doors. This does not work well with VUIs. You need to trust the user's grasp of the language and move forward. Trust goes both ways, where the assistant trusts the user to know how to set an alarm and the user knows that the assistant will help out if the user finds it too difficult.

Check out the example shown in Figure 2-3.

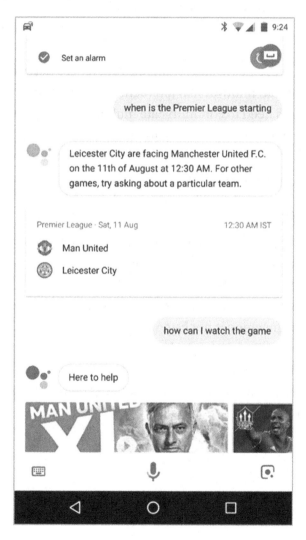

Figure 2-3. *Google Assistant provides more information than the literal question asked*

This is an excellent example of maintaining context and cooperating with the user. Google Assistant could have simply told the date the Premier league starts, but instead it gave the name of the teams and the time it starts. It even gave me a guided clue to continue the conversation. This is a subtler way of continuing a conversation instead of asking a second question. The user feels that sense of freedom.

When asked a second question, it maintains context and gives a specific answer.

At this point, we need to understand the differences between pure voice interactions and multi-modal interactions (GUI+VUI).

When there is a need to communicate multiple types of data to a user and you have a screen, use it; show a card in the case of Google Assistant. A card is generally designed for easy consumption and is the most efficient way of grouping relevant data. The user's need to anthropomorphize is greater in pure VUIs, as it feels like a phone call because we try to find a person behind that voice.

The visual component can allow the user to continue at a more leisurely pace. In an IVR, it is difficult to pause the system—instead, the user must continually interact, which is a problem because users want to be in control of the system all the time. The feeling that we are no longer in control and the machine is not listening or behaving the way he/she wanted it to becomes frustrating and erodes trust. Take advantage of the extra medium whenever possible but regardless, there is a difference in expectation when a human is talking to a human and when he/she is talking to a device.

Taken from Google's blog on Duplex:[3]

> "When people talk to each other, they use more
> complex sentences than when talking to computers.
> They correct themselves mid-sentence, are more
> verbose, or omit words and rely on context instead;
> they also express a wide range of intents, sometimes
> in the same sentence, e.g., "So umm Tuesday
> through Thursday we are open 11 to 2, and then
> reopen 4 to 9, and then Friday, Saturday, Sunday
> we... or Friday, Saturday we're open 11 to 9 and then
> Sunday we're open 1 to 9."

In natural spontaneous speech, people talk faster and less clearly than they do when they speak to a machine. The problem is aggravated during phone calls, which often have loud background noises and sound quality issues.

In longer conversations, the same sentence can have very different meanings depending on the context. For example, when booking reservations "Yes, 4" can mean the time of the reservation or the number of people. Often the relevant context might be several sentences back, a problem that gets compounded by the increased word error rate in phone calls.

Progressive Disclosure

Progressive disclosure is an interaction design technique often used in human computer interaction to help maintain the focus of a user's attention by reducing clutter, confusion, and cognitive workload. This improves usability by presenting only the minimum data required for the task at hand. See Figure 2-2.

---

[3]Leviathan, Yaniv; Matias, Yossi; "Google Duplex: An AI System for Accomplishing Real-World Tasks Over the Phone," Google AIBlog, May 8, 2018, https://ai. googleblog.com/2018/05/duplex-ai-system-for-natural-conversation.html.

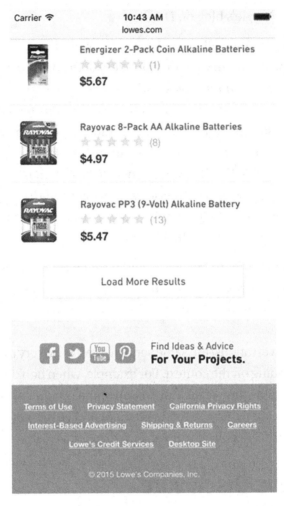

Figure 2-4. *An example of progressive disclosure, whereby only a few battery options are shown at first*

Let's look at the same example first:

Me: Max, what can you do for me?

Max: I can set alarms, timers, lists, and reminders, track flights, packages, news, sports, movies, play games, and tell jokes.

A human cannot remember more than three options at once when he/she has not paid full attention. Besides, how can we expect someone to remember everything? We simply can't. This is where progressive disclosure plays a big part. Do not give more than three-four options at once and indicate that the user has to ask for more if they want it.

> Me: Max, what can you do for me?

> Max: I can set alarms for you. I can also set reminders for you. Do you want to hear some more things I can do?

This problem becomes even more evident when I am exploring options to buy. Just imagine my assistant talking about every specification of every laptop after I ask *Max, I want to buy a laptop. Show me some options.*

This model works well in GUIs too, as opposed to showing a flat infinite list. Once you click on Load More, the user becomes emotionally invested to explore more options. See Figure 2-5.

Figure 2-5. *GUI interfaces also use progressive disclosure*

Progressive disclosure might add a few steps to your design, but that's not always a bad thing. Use it correctly and you'll have a powerful technique to keeps your designs focused.

Variety

Look at this example:

> Sunday 7AM
>
> *Me: How are you?*
>
> *Max: I am good.*
>
> Monday 10PM
>
> *Me: How are you?*
>
> *Max: I am good.*
>
> Thursday 7PM
>
> *Me: How are you?*
>
> *Max: I am good.*

Humans do not talk like this. It's because we are not programmed linearly. We relish variety. Humans are maybe the only species with the concept of boredom. So, you need to randomize. For any given prompt, there are usually a few conversational alternatives that'll work. Focus your efforts on prompts that users hear frequently, so these phrases don't become tiresome. Let's see how this conversation turns out using this principle.

> Sunday 7AM
>
> *Me: How are you?*
>
> *Max: I am good, sunbathing right now in my digital space.*
>
> Monday 10PM
>
> *Me: How are you?*
>
> *Max: Right now, I am happy because you enjoyed your trip to Greece.*

A simpler example would be a person asking what time it is. You can respond with "it's eleven in the morning", "its 11o'clock", or "its 11am to be exact."

Give and Take

It is all about taking turns in a multi-turn conversation. Turn-taking is about who has the "mic"—taking the mic, holding the mic, and handing it over to another speaker. To manage this complex process, we rely on a rich inventory of cues embedded in sentence structure, including intonation, eye gaze, and body language. Take a Google Action for example, which will be limited in expressing and detecting these cues. You can still write prompts in a way that helps the user know when to take their turn. Or imagine using Alexa to set a reminder. First you need to say that you want the task of setting a reminder done, then Alexa asks you about the details, and then finally asks for the time and date of the reminder.

Let's look at this example to see how this can be explained:

Me: Set a reminder.

Max: What's the reminder?

Me: Buy eggs.

Max: Okay, buy eggs. When do you want to be reminded?

Me: Tomorrow at 10am.

Me: Sure, I'll remind you tomorrow at 10am.

When humans talk, they take turns, where the "right" to speak flips back and forth between partners. This conversational pitter-patter is so familiar and seemingly unremarkable that we rarely remark on it. But consider the timing: On average, each turn lasts for around two seconds, and the typical gap between them is just 200 milliseconds—barely enough time to utter a syllable. That figure is nigh-universal. It exists across cultures, with only slight variations. It's even there in sign language conversations. "It's the minimum human response time to anything," says Stephen Levinson from the Max Planck Institute for Psycholinguistics. Levinson describes this as a "basic metabolism of human social life"—a universal tendency to minimize the silence between turns, without overlaps.

Even great apes like chimps take turns when gesturing to each other and other primates. Several monkeys and one species of lemur take turns when calling. One team of researchers recently showed that pairs of common marmosets leave predictable gaps of five to six seconds between turns and will match a partner's rhythm if it speeds up or slows down. These simian see-saws could be independent innovations, or they could reflect an ancient framework that we humans built on when we evolved the capacity for speech.

In general, two people speaking try to help each other. And to a remarkable degree, they succeed. For example, there are some words that are generally considered conversational detritus: "uh", "um", and "mm-hmm". "Uh" and "um" signal to the other speaker that a turn is not quite finished; that the speaker is planning something more. This makes sense only in the light of the split-second timing with which speakers take turns. Men use these pause-fillers more than women, being perhaps more eager to hold the floor. (For unknown reasons, they also prefer "uh" and women prefer "um".) Those who tend not to use "um" and "uh" often replace it with something else, like "so," which is much derided as meaningless at the beginning of a statement.

Like "um" and "uh," the humble "mm-hmm" and "uh-huh" are critical too. Listeners use them to show they have understood the speaker and are sympathetic. To show their importance, researchers concocted a devilish experiment in which speakers were asked to tell about a near-death experience, while listeners were given a distracting task like pressing a button every time the speaker used a word starting with "T". As a result, the listener was less able to encourage the speaker with "mm-hmm". This drove the speakers themselves to distraction. They paused more, used more "ums" and "uhs" themselves, and repeated the dramatic lines of their stories, desperate for affirmation that they had been understood.

From a certain point of view, what is fascinating about conversation is not how hard it is, but how well people subconsciously cooperate to make it seem easy.

Moving Forward

In this chapter, we saw that we need to be mindful of the intricacies of conversation. Every conversation has a purpose, either completing a task or being entertained. Each of these conversations need flows and these pieces have to be designed in a natural and instinctive way. For intent-based conversations, every turn is an opportunity to drive the conversation to the logical goal of completing the task. We need to set user expectations for the product.

In the next chapter, we talk about personality—whether we need it, and if yes, how we go about designing it.

CHAPTER 3

Personality

"There is no such thing as a voice user interface with no personality."

—Cohen, Giangola, and Balogh, 2004[1]

Now that we have discussed the principles of VUI in Chapter 2, we are moving on to the topic of personality. In this chapter, we learn whether we need personality and how to design for it.

As stated in Chapter 2, humans attribute intentionality and mental states to living and nonliving entities, a phenomenon known as *anthropomorphism.* Anthropomorphism is defined as the attribution of human characteristics or behavior to a nonhuman entity in the environment. It includes phenomena as diverse as attributing thoughts and emotions.

To some, it is considered a universal human trait to anthropomorphize the relevant subjects and objects in one's environment.

In the article "The Mind Behind Anthropomorphic Thinking: Attribution of Mental States to Other Species",[2] the authors Esmeralda G. Urquiza-Haas and Kurt Kotrschal argue that anthropomorphism has

---

[1]Cohen, Michael H., Giangola, James P., Balogh, Jennifer; *Voice User Interface Design,* O'Reilly, 2004.

[2]Urquiza-Hass, Esmeralda; Kotrschal, Kurt; "The Mind Behind Anthropomorphic Thinking: Attribution of Mental States to Other Species," *Animal Behavior,* vol 109, Nov 2015, pp 167-176.

also been proposed to be a result of a cognitive default state. The main idea behind this hypothesis is that the human brain evolved to efficiently process social information. Within this framework, anthropomorphism emerges as an automatic response to any human-like behavior (Caporael & Heyes, 1997)[3] or human-like feature (Guthrie, 1997)[4] that requires a swift identification or interpretation, which cannot be accounted for using the knowledge at hand.

"Mirror Neurons" is a fascinating TED Talk by neuroscientist Vilayanur Ramachandran[5] about the function of and evidence for mirror neurons. He argues that this neuropsychological mechanism has shaped human evolution and particularly our interactions with each other in society. Dr. Ramachandran argues that mirror neurons might be a key to understanding how and why people seem to be able to so quickly identify with and react emotionally and intensely to avatars, which are—after all—really just pixels flashing rapidly on a screen.

These studies point to an overarching human behavior where we associate human emotions to try to understand a complex object. This has happened gradually through natural selection where a living being who is more alert would survive and the one who is not will eventually perish. We can argue that this might be one of the vital reasons why humans have survived natural selection and not gone extinct as a species. These are the neurons that shaped civilization.

---

[3]Caporael, LR; Heyes, CM; "Why Anthropomorphize? Folk Psychology and Other Stories," in Mitchell, R, et al., eds, *Anthropomorphism, Anecdotes, and Animals,* Suny Press, 1997, pp 59-73.

[4]Guthrie, SE; "Anthropomorphism: a Definition and a Theory," in Mitchell, R, et al., eds, *Anthropomorphism, Anecdotes, and Animals,* Suny Press, 1997, pp 50-58.

[5]TEDIndia 2009, https://www.ted.com/talks/vs_ramachandran_the_neurons _that_shaped_civilization

We can see the same behavior in every object we see around us. A simplified, unscientific verification of the phenomenon can be seen in this example (see Figures 3-1 and 3-2).

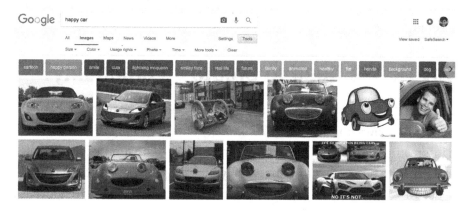

Figure 3-1. *A simplified unscientific verification of the phenomenon*

Figure 3-2. *A simplified unscientific verification of the phenomenon*

Humans really want to understand the world around them, even it is too complex for them to do so. They find the next-best approach. They project a personality to the object and try to read it. The objects that humans interact the most in their lives are other people. And they put in more effort studying those faces; trying to understand how they feel, their thoughts, and so on. This is a survival instinct.

41

This is applicable to disembodied voices too. Suppose a stranger calls you on the phone today. Immediately, you will create a persona for that voice. You will start with gender, then you will make assumptions about age, height, weight, etc. The same happens when we interact with a voice assistant.

Why Do We Need to Create a Personality?

Users will assign a personality whether we have designed it or not. Leonard Klie, Senior News Editor, *Speech Technology* and *CRM* magazines, has an interesting take on it:[6] The bottom line for most consumers, though, is that despite enormous investments by the companies that are trying to get—or keep—their business, they would rather talk to a warm body than a cold computer. Many have expressed anger at a cold computer that is pretending to be anything but. An entire blog, for example, has been devoted to complaints about Virgin Mobile USA's Simone character.

"What makes it so odd is not just that they try to make it sound like Simone is a real person. It isn't even that they try to make Simone a clear and vivid character. It's that they go through all this effort, then make it transparently apparent that Simone is simply a computer program," one frustrated blogger wrote.

"It's always her, and she always says the same lines the same way. I guess it's a little more friendly and distinctive than the standard 'PLEASE. ENTER. YOUR. TEN. DIGIT. CODE. NOW.' bit, but it's disorienting. Is this somebody's attempt to seem 'hip' or what?" asked another.

For many customers, though, a little personality is better than none at all. One writer on a blog devoted to Bell Canada's Emily penned the following: "She may be annoying, but she's a far sight better than the

---

[6]Klie, Leonard; "It's a Persona, Not a Personality," *Speech Technology*. June 1, 2017, http://www.speechtechmag.com/Articles/Editorial/Feature/Its-a-Persona-Not-a-Personality-36311.aspx

50 different phone numbers all leading to different touchtone menus that Bell had before. No matter how much we might want it, they're just not going to hire enough real, live people to answer all those calls.

The whole question is whether or not we try to humanize a bot, but what happens when a human realizes that it is a bot? There are levels to it. We review these levels in the following sections.

Users Know That They Are Talking to a Voice Assistant Who Helps Get Things Done

In this case, it is not about assigning a personality, it is about making the interaction easier and more natural. This is why Google has not given a name to its voice assistant like Microsoft or Amazon did. They want to keep it as neutral as possible, but keep the interaction, the conversation, authentic. The voice represents the entire company, not just the assistant. You are interacting with a virtual face of the company. It matters whether you can get things done easily or not. A voice should mirror the image of the brand and the company.

A voice assistant by, say LinkedIn, is not expected to be chatty and careless. Eros Marcello, a senior Conversational AI Specialist for Alexa, Amazon has an interesting perspective:[7]

> "Your personality should come out in the design, not in the agent. Chances are, your employer or client has distinct expectations—perhaps even a formulated style guide—that their conversational

---

[7]Newlands, Murray; "10 Essential Tips on Voice User Interface Design for AI," *Forbes*, Aug 25, 2017, https://www.forbes.com/sites/mnewlands/2017/08/25/10-essential-tips-on-voice-user-interface-design-for-ai/#7de13e722422

agents' persona must adhere to. You'll find that there's often little to no room to be creative in your sense of the word. You're not crafting content for your podcast or blog. You're concocting an interactive experience laced with potent branding. Infusing your own personality into the agent isn't the point. Your personality is showcased in cunning design decision, unique workflow, impactful execution in adherence to the stakeholder, and most of all, in your ability to marry functionality with an enriching experience for the end user."

Users Know That They Are Talking to a Voice Assistant When They Are Also Interacting with a Screen (Multi-Modal)

If the GUI elements do not complement those of the voice, then creating a killer VUI will inherently prove to be a fruitless endeavor. This brings us to avatars, or the visual representation of a digital assistant. Then comes the next question: *Do we want a face or something more abstract?*

Cortana's writers spent a lot of time thinking about her personality:[8]

"Our approach on personality includes defining a voice with an actual personality. This included writing a detailed personality and laying out how we wanted Cortana to be perceived. We used words like witty, confident, and loyal to describe how Cortana responds through voice, text, and animated

---

[8]Ash, Marcus; "How Cortana Comes to Life in Windows 10," Microsoft Cortana Blog, Feb 10, 2015, https://blogs.windows.com/windowsexperience/2015/02/10/how-cortana-comes-to-life-in-windows-10/

character. We wrote an actual script based on this definition that is spoken by a trained voice actress with thousands of responses to questions that will have variability to make Cortana feel like it has an actual personality and isn't just programmed with robotic responses."

Suppose we want a face for the personality. There are two things to consider: it should appeal to target users and it should not be even remotely offensive.

Next, the avatar can be static or dynamic. Chatbots generally use a static avatar. For Microsoft Ruuh, they created an avatar that targets their user segment—the young population. Ruuh should also be a friend and someone you can talk freely with. You can chat with Ruuh anytime, on any topic. It is super friendly. Everyone desires a friend with whom they can open up to. But there's something that stops us from being completely frank!

Lack of trust or the fear that your conversations can go viral can be some of the reasons. You can trust Ruuh on this point. You cannot have a secret keeper better than Ruuh (see Figure 3-3).

Figure 3-3. *The Ruuh chatbot avatar*

For digital assistants with a GUI presence, this becomes more interesting when they have the option to animate. Here, the assistant will behave like a human; they will listen to your question, think, answer back, make a joke, sing, show sadness and anger, and lots of other emotions. These can be portrayed using animations. For reference, check out the abstract avatar representations by Google Assistant or Cortana (see Figure 3-4).

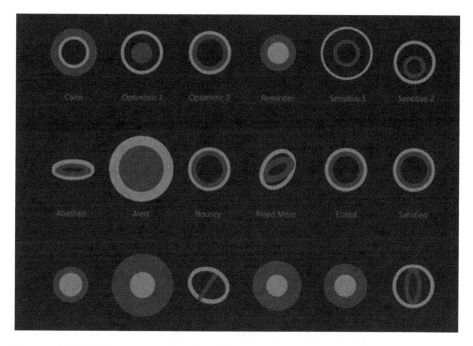

Figure 3-4. *The many moods of Cortana*

The first thing you might notice from this example is that companies try not to create an avatar or personality that is intimidating. This text is not meant to go into the technical aspect of it, but we know that creating a virtual digital assistant needs a lot of AI and Machine Learning (ML) support with Natural Language (NL) capabilities. We do not want that to be obvious while users are interacting with the avatar. The avatar needs to be simple, fun, and trustworthy.

If users know that they are interacting with a virtual entity, digital assistants should not try to be perceived as human. However, they should use small details of human interaction in every turn so that users can identify with the behavior and interact with the system more openly and easily.

Let's take the example of Sophia (see Figure 3-5). Sophia is a social humanoid robot developed by Hong Kong-based company Hanson Robotics. Sophia has a humanoid face with expressions. She shows emotions when responding as well. But humans have evolved to perceive emotions very naturally and any expression that's not completely consistent with the intended response is extremely easy to spot. Now, this is not the responsibility of the designer of the conversation, but the person who designed the body language and expressions as Sophia's responses to human questions. There is a lack of consistency that becomes very uncomfortable as one talks to her.

Figure 3-5. *Sophia is a social humanoid robot*

Humans use a lot of microexpressions for emoting as well (see Figure 3-6). A microexpression is the result of a voluntary or involuntary emotional response that conflicts with another. This results in the individual very briefly displaying their true emotions followed by a false emotional reaction. Human emotions are an unconscious bio-psycho-social reaction that derives from the amygdala, the body's alarm circuit for fear, which lies in an almond-shaped mass of nuclei deep in the brain's temporal lobe. The amygdala, from the Greek word for almond, controls autonomic responses associated with fear, arousal, and emotional stimulation. These microexpressions typically last .5-4 seconds, although they usually last less than half of a second.

Figure 3-6. *Human micro expressions*

These expressions need to be portrayed by a realistic avatar too. Otherwise, it just becomes difficult for users to associate with it and build a relationship. It does not feel authentic and users may feel cheated by the whole experience. One needs to be mindful of the fact that the assistant should come across as simple, helpful, and human-like in its attitude. It should understand its own limitations. In a few years, we should be ready to build a better Sophia and it will become the eventual norm, but we still have a ways to go.

Users Do Not Know That They Are Talking to a Voice Assistant

In recent years, we have seen a revolution in the ability of computers to understand and generate natural speech, with the full application of deep neural networks (Google voice search and WaveNet). Still, it is often frustrating having to talk to computerized voices that don't understand natural language. In particular, automated phone systems are still struggling to recognize simple words and commands. They force the caller to adjust to the system instead of the system adjusting to the caller. There are many scenarios like customer support, booking appointments, or organizing an event where we have to call real people on the phone and do multiple tasks. These are opportunities where a virtual assistant can increase productivity.

Google recently announced Google Duplex, a new technology for conducting natural conversations to carry out tasks like booking appointments over the phone. For such tasks, the system makes the conversational experience as natural as possible, allowing people to speak normally, like they would to another person, without having to adapt to a machine. But there is one missing link—the person on the other side does not know that they are speaking to a virtual entity. There has actually been a lot of argument on the ethics of doing something like this, as people need to know who they are actually talking to.

One of the key research insights for Google Duplex was to constrain it to closed/narrow domains, which are deep enough to explore extensively. The system can carry out natural conversations after being deeply trained in such domains. It cannot carry out general conversations. This only happens with a lot of ML training that processes huge amounts of caller data.

Suppose we are designing Max for this intent. First, we do it in phases. We select domains based on user need, market appeal, data availability, and a host of different factors and start getting deeper. We build answers for a host of queries regarding the said domain, say "handling real-world tasks". We go deep in this domain.

Next, we build similar networks (see Figure 3-7) for the selected domains, say for sports, daily routines, news, casual conversation, and your social life. Our Max can now answer any queries about any sports team in the world. He knows about all the upcoming matches, previous tournaments, and sports trivia. We can have a natural conversation with Max about sports.

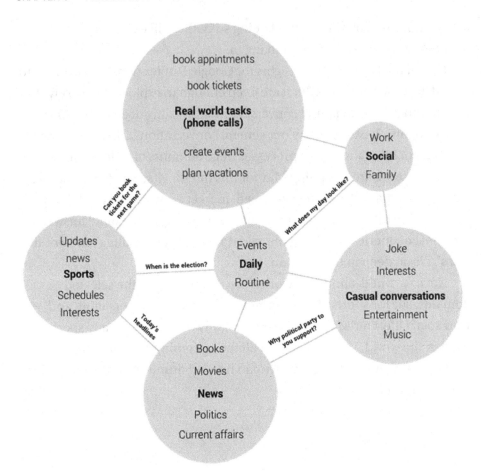

Figure 3-7. *Building networks*

Now these domains are independent. These domains then need to be connected to some queries, which connect the dots. These queries are conversation links. "Can you book tickets for the next game?" Now, Max can book tickets, as he has been trained to handle queries in this domain. See Figure 3-7.

Max, while conversing with you, can direct the whole conversation from one domain to the next to appear more humanlike.

Let's take an example:

> *Me: Max, when is Barcelona playing Real Madrid next?*
>
> *Max: Barcelona is playing Real Madrid next on 28th of this month. I see that you have a business trip in Barcelona at that time. Do you want me to book tickets?*
>
> *Me: Oh yes! I had completely forgotten about the trip.*
>
> *Max: Would you like me to book a single ticket?*
>
> *Me: Yes, please.*

In this conversation, Max shifted from one domain to another seamlessly by connecting the two domains (booking tickets). The user was genuinely surprised by Max's intelligence, as Max had to connect the dots between sports news, the work calendar, flight tickets, and booking capability.

In this small example, you see the principles detailed in the previous chapter (such as personalization, leveraging context, and understanding intent) all coming into play.

With time, these domains get used more and more by users and with time, we have a huge dataset to train the assistant even more. Max will gradually become an expert in these domains.

Next, we gradually widen the net of the interconnecting queries and increase the playing field (see Figure 3-8). What this does is increase the variety with which Max shifts domains; Max can actually start getting better in these secondary domains and can gradually become a fully developed assistant with whom you can have a natural conversation. See Figure 3-8.

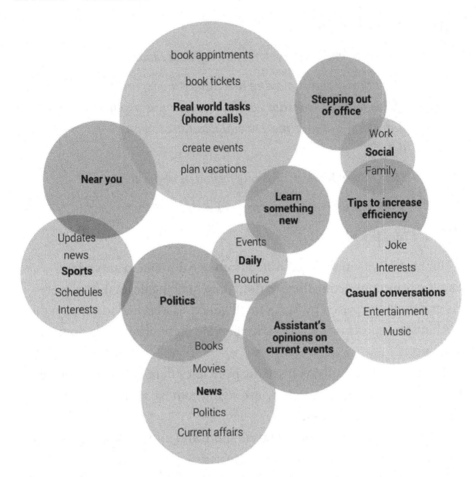

Figure 3-8. *Example of interconnections*

Gradually, Max will have deeper conversations about events, news near you, and politics, and will be able to learn new skills and suggest tips to increase efficiency. For example, "stepping out of office" might be a simple scenario but to actually execute it requires a deeper understanding of the possibilities and consequences that need to be handled by Max.

Now Max can handle six new domains to support the initial six hero domains. In these, we see multiple places where Max would need to do real-world tasks, interacting with other people. Also, he needs to sound and behave like a human, supposing we go with the Duplex model.

The Duplex model is extremely interesting because the assistant did two things which were entirely different from what other assistants have been doing.

Using Hesitation Markers

N.J. Enfield, a professor of linguistics at the University of Sydney, calls the process of receiving a question, analyzing it, searching for an answer, coming up with the exact sentence, and responding to the said question as a "conversation machine." In his book *How We Talk*,[9] he examines how conversational minutiae—filler words like "um" and "mm-hmm" and pauses that are longer than 200 milliseconds—grease the wheels of this machine. If you ask difficult questions, the responses are delayed as there is more data to process. In these instances, humans tend to use hesitation markers like "umm" and "uh". These responses before the actual response have no content but they generally infer, "Wait please, because I know time's ticking and I don't want to leave silence but I'm not ready to produce what I want to say." Not just this, there is also another reason why we use these markers. These are used in instances when we do not agree with what the other person said, or prefer a different take on the matter. An example of this would be, "Let's have dinner outside tonight". If I am not free, the response comes out slower, but we fill the space in between with a filler "Umm, I am busy today, how about tomorrow evening?" These is no processing delay in this, but we are made aware that this response was not expected by the other person. It is also a signal that the person has listened to what you just said and now it is their turn to respond. Basically, "hand over the mic".

---

[9]https://www.theatlantic.com/science/archive/2017/12/the-secret-life-of-um/547961/

Adding Pauses

While conversing, humans mostly follow the rule of "No gap, no overlap." But the interesting part here is that the time we take to process ultimately reveals that we are humans. Suppose I ask "When will you be free this weekend?" and you reply, "I will be free from 1-3 this Saturday and from 4-7 this Sunday" and you take about 600 milliseconds to respond. This does not sound natural because although humans take about the same time—about 600 milliseconds—to come up with what they want to say, this question demanded thought before replying. It takes time to process your calendar and then come up with the response. We take longer pauses before we speak when we have to think.

The ideal response would be "Well, <silence: 400 milliseconds> (thinking: I have gym in the morning and then the music class), I will be free around 1 this Saturday, and approximately around 4 on Sunday." Notice the difference between the two responses. There are two distinct differences: variety in response and pauses. Here, the word "well" becomes the hesitation marker.

Everything relates to this simple quote:

"The cues in voice seem uniquely humanizing..."[10]

---

[10]Schroeder, J; Epley, N: "Mistaking Minds and Machines: How Speech Affects Dehumanization and Anthropomorphism," *Journal of Experimental Psychology: General,* Aug 11, 2016.

Personality is broken into statistically-identified factors called the *big five*[11]—openness to experience, conscientiousness, extroversion, agreeableness, and neuroticism (or emotional stability). Let's look at each one in more detail:

- **Openness to experience**—Described as the extent to which a person is imaginative or independent and depicts a personal preference for a variety of activities over a strict routine. This could include appreciation for art, emotion, adventure, unusual ideas, curiosity, and variety of experiences.

- **Conscientiousness (efficient/organized vs easy-going/careless)**—The personality trait of being careful or vigilant. Conscientiousness implies a desire to do a task well and to take obligations to others seriously.

- **Extroversion**—A central dimension of human personality. Extraversion tends to be manifested in outgoing, talkative, energetic behavior, whereas introversion is manifested in more reserved and solitary behavior.

- **Agreeableness**—A personality trait manifesting itself in individual behavioral characteristics that are perceived as kind, sympathetic, cooperative, warm, and considerate.

- **Neuroticism**—Also refers to the degree of emotional stability and impulse control. It can be considered as a differentiation between sensitive/nervous vs secure/confident trait of a human being.

---

[11]Sutin, AR, et al.; "The five-factor model of personality and physical inactivity; a meta analysis of 16 samples," *Journal of Research in Personality*, vol 63, Aug 2016, pp 22-28.

To design a personality for your assistant, these five factors need to be addressed. It is like creating an imaginary world where you are designing the expression of an emotion. For this, let's jump from intent-based conversation to casual conversation. This is a world where users are talking to your voice assistant without any intent or purpose. They just want to have a conversation, very similar to talking to an actual person.

We also need to consider single turn vs multi-turn conversations. Single-turn conversations are the conversations where the user asks a question and the assistant responds with an answer and stops listening. The user needs to invoke the assistant again to continue. For example:

> *Me: Hey Max, what is your favorite movie?*
>
> *Max: I just love things from the past; so yeah, I love Jurassic Park, Raawwwrr.*
>
> *Me: Hey Max, have you seen a dinosaur?*

The user had to invoke Max each time before querying. In multi-turn conversations, either Max has the listening mode on, or Max guides you to a second question casually and keeps the listening mode on. For example:

> *Me: Hey Max, what is your favorite movie?*
>
> *Max: I just love things from the past; so yeah, I love Jurassic Park, Raawwwrr. Have you seen the movie?*
>
> *Me: Yes, I have! Have you seen a dinosaur?*

Now, coming to the personality aspect of it, it is your call whether you want the assistant to be easy going, helpful, angry, responsible, etc. Suppose you have a tech limitation and you do not have context—you don't know where the user is, the user's activities, or the user's current emotional state. It may be due to lack of data on your part or anything else. Now, it is difficult to react to a situation as you are not aware of what the user is going through.

Suppose I say, "Hey Max, how was your day?" In this scenario, if you were talking to a friend, he/she could guess the emotional state you are in and respond accordingly. But, in this scenario, Max has no idea how the user's day was. And suppose that the user had a really bad day and Max responds "Today was the best day of my virtual life". This doesn't sound empathetic, does it?

Generally, humans tend to mirror emotions for various purposes. Mirroring is the behavior in which a person subconsciously imitates the gesture, speech pattern, or attitude of another. Mirroring often occurs in social situations, particularly in the company of close friends or family. It helps to facilitate empathy, as individuals more readily experience other people's emotions through mimicking posture and gestures. This empathy may help individuals create lasting relationships and thus excel in social situations. The action of mirroring allows individuals to believe they are more similar to another person, and perceived similarity can be the basis for creating a relationship. Now with just audio being the medium, it becomes all the more important to mirror emotions. The user needs to feel that Max is understanding what he says. He needs to feel that Max can be trusted. Suppose that Max knows that the user had a long day with a series of meetings. Max should probably reply like this:

> *Me: Hey Max, how was your day?*
>
> *Max: It has been a long day today working on my AI. But I feel better now talking with you.*

This apparent projection of empathy is extremely important to increase the feeling of trust between the user and Max. Max projects empathy but doesn't get bogged down and gives a positive twist to the whole conversation. It is Max's job to make the user feel good.

This can be done even with intent-based conversation. Say, I am asking Max, "Remind me to wish dad happy birthday tomorrow at 11:55 PM." Max can understand that it's a reminder about a birthday; the second entity here is "dad". So, Max can respond "I will remind you of that and do wish him on my behalf too". This might sound creepy to some, as we do not yet find it commonplace for our assistants to do these things. But it is bound to happen in the near future, when voice becomes a more comfortable medium of interaction between humans and machines.

In most scenarios today, we would hardly work toward this result for casual assistant conversations. We would have a set of answers for a particular type of question and Max would give one of his built-in responses. For this, the responses need to be balanced and should not portray strong emotions. The stronger the projected emotion, the stronger might be the reaction from the user. And in this case, it does not mirror the other way since the user knows that he is talking to a machine. The user will talk slowly and make sure the assistant responds; they will generally not show or mirror emotion consciously. So, if the assistant is portraying a higher level of happiness and the user cannot relate to that emotion, the user will get irritated. It is about showing openness and clear thoughts, showcasing information, and offering support. Taking the same example forward, see Figure 3-9.

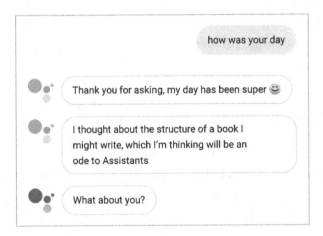

Figure 3-9. *Google assistant*

In Figure 3-9, Google assistant portrays exactly what has been mentioned. It shows openness, displays a bit of humor as a part of its personality, and ends with a question asking the same. This is a simplified version of mirroring.

Google also uses emojis as it has a chat surface and it humanizes the conversation, similar to how a friend usually responds on these platforms.

We are designing to evoke emotional responses from users to virtual entities. The bottom line for most users is that despite enormous investments by the companies that are trying to get—or keep—their business, they would rather talk to a warm body than a cold computer. Many have even expressed anger at a cold computer that is pretending to be anything but.

In order to know Max and develop a relationship of friendliness and trust, the user will try to know whether their interests and personalities align. This leads to another aspect of personality—showcasing opinions and preferences. Users will ask about politics, sports, movies, entertainment, music, food, and anything under the sun. Creating a distinct and stable personality whose preferences remain consistent and do not become unpredictable is important. This is because we are creating a distinct persona that a user can relate to, something based on their existing mental models. So it needs to be grounded in reality, in today's culture and values. To showcase distinct opinions, one needs to be mindful of ethics.

- What happens when a user is directing inappropriate behavior toward the assistant? How should it respond?

- What happens when a user is asking which candidate it supports? We should not utilize our influence to affect elections and rules of the state.

- What happens when a user asks questions about the assistant's identity regarding race and gender?

The easiest way to dissolve these situations is by reminding the user that the assistant is not a human, rather a virtual manifestation. It helps to divert the topic to something funny and stay neutral in positions of influence. It is easier said than done when you know that the assistant has the potential to bring about a positive change in behavior. Regarding this, I show two examples. See Figures 3-10 and 3-11.

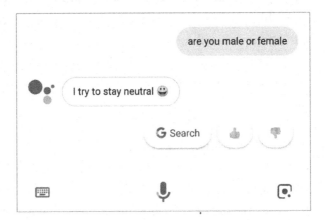

Figure 3-10. *Google assistant*

Figure 3-11. *Cortana response to 'F*** you'*

In this scenario, it literally tries to stay neutral. Favoritism from AI will alienate a bunch of users from your experience. But coming back to the question as to whether we want to change user's behavior or not—Google and Alexa have taken an interesting stance where they reward users verbally for addressing the assistant with "please" and "thank you". Google provides this option for kids to improve their behavior. I will not give any opinion on the feature, but I would like you to think how this affects the user's emotions.

- Google has planned to include phrases like "Pretty please" and "thank you" when interacting with kids to inculcate a better behavior. "Pretty please" might be an instant but can this be the step in the door for all experiences where it can influence our behavior?

- Whose responsibility is it to inculcate good behavior in individuals?

- How does this affect the personality of the assistant from the perspective of the user? Does it sound caring or controlling?

- Where do we draw the line and say, this is where we stop giving our opinions?

- Is it divulging the secret that the assistant isn't real, no one is perfect, and everybody has flaws? Is it the assistant being more polite than is believable?

- Where do we draw the line to say Max will showcase that it's an AI and not a human with flaws? If it does showcase in all instances that it is an AI manifestation, then does it need to be responsible for a person's behavior at all?

Cortana's take on this issue has been different until now (see Figure 3-11).

Me: F*** you

Cortana: Moving on...

From this response, we see that Cortana understands what has been said, does not pretend to not hear it, and then without judging the user, simply diverts the topic.

There is one more reason why it is important to keep the personality of your assistant balanced and not too well defined. Personality indicates that the object has preferences and interests; it would do a certain set of things but never do other things. Suppose I create Max such that he loves movies, is easy going, likes to have fun, and is an overall friend who generally likes the brighter side of life and takes interest in popular culture. Now, imagine in few years' time, you, being the creator of Max, see the opportunity that Max has the data and technological skillset to become a great bank assistant. Now, a bank is a completely different domain where Max has the ability to crunch numbers, support user queries. Customers will come and fulfill their banking needs by interacting with Max. He has the ability to process huge amounts of data, forecast project growth, and give suggestions. Basically, he's an ideal assistant for financial institutions.

Will you, after having built the personality for Max, allow him to be this kind of assistant as well? Will it suit his personality? Will users take Max seriously?

Will people accept the friendly home assistant as the one managing his/her money?

It is very different job from daily household tasks. It is not like an oven, which you can use at home as well as in a small restaurant. This oven has flexibility about where it can work.

Moving Forward

In this chapter, we saw when and why our voice AI needs a personality. We also saw how deep we need to go to start building one. Now we have an idea how users react to different types of responses, and know when and how to give opinions. We also went deeper into casual conversations or conversations with no intent, per se.

In the next chapter, we talk further about intent-based conversations, which are conversations we do to carry out a task with a very definite intent. We will consider scenarios and see how the experience can be made smoother.

CHAPTER 4

The Power of Multi-Modal Interactions

In the previous chapters, we discussed the various methods of understanding and creating a voice-based interaction. We saw several examples of how a voice-based user interface would respond to various use cases.

If you have actually interacted with a voice-based user interface, you have noticed how there are always other ways to interact with the systems in case the VUI is unable to understand the user's intent. Often, most user interface systems allow multiple inputs or ways for the user to interact with the system. This ability for a user to interact with the system in multiple ways is known as *multi-modal interaction,* or simply multiple modes of interaction.

In real-world scenarios, human beings perceive the world through their multiple senses—touch, smell, sight, hearing, and taste—while acting on these inputs through their effectors—limbs, eyes, body, and voice.

Similar to human senses, computers (devices) use inputs from various sensors to communicate or implement commands given by the humans. They use keyboards, microphones, cameras, and, more recently, touchscreens. There are two types of channels to communicate—sensors and effectors. As the name suggests, sensors are used to detect input for the system, while effectors are used to give output for the system.

© Ritwik Dasgupta 2018
R. Dasgupta, *Voice User Interface Design*, https://doi.org/10.1007/978-1-4842-4125-7_4

Even a voice-based interaction or speech detection is dependent on a device having a good capable microphone to catch/record the instructions from the users.

In any human-computer interaction, when the system uses two or more modes of communication, this is known as a multi-modal interaction. One may ask why you would need two methods to communicate with the system. Let's explain this using the following example:

Our AI assistant was placed in a user's mobile device. The user was travelling to a crowded metro are, and the user suddenly remembered that on their way back they must not forget to pick up groceries. The user would like Max to help him set a reminder. There is only one problem— it's a crowded metro full of noise and other commuters speaking to each other. No matter how hard you try, Max just can't figure out the call to action. In a regular case we could have simply called out to our assistant, by saying, "Hey Max, create a reminder to get groceries after work today". Unfortunately, the ambient noise in the current system is just too much.

So, what would you do? Forget about the groceries, or just set a reminder by typing it using your assistant? In most cases, the user will simply type out a reminder on the chat interface of the AI assistant to be able to complete the task.

Until quite recently, computers, mobiles, and other devices that have become a part of our daily routines were constrained by the abilities of the devices themselves, i.e., the hardware or software used by the device. This meant that users essentially were confined to the limit of the interactions of the interface available on the device. The hardware has slowly been changing over the past few years where devices have become much more capable, thanks to the many gigabytes of RAM, higher processing power, lower battery consumption, and smaller sizes available to them. These have allowed the software to be able to perform more tasks.

HCI (human computer interaction) has been around for quite some time—even as early as the early 1950s, with punch cards for data storage and input. Initially the only people who interacted with the computers were information technology professionals and dedicated hobbyists. This changed disruptively with the introduction of the personal computer in the late 1980s. The focus was then on personal computing. Software, such as text editors and spreadsheets, made almost everybody in the world a potential computer user and also revealed the inherent deficiencies of computers with respect to usability.

HCI incorporated cognitive psychology, artificial intelligence, and philosophy of mind, to articulate systematic and scientifically informed applications to be known as cognitive engineering. It allowed people with concepts, skills, and a vision to address the practical needs of human computer interaction.

HCI has always been facilitated by analogous developments in engineering and design areas adjacent to HCI, including human factors, engineering, and documentation development. Some of the important early examples of computer interfaces date from as early as the late 18th century. Let's look at a list of important evolutions in human computer interactions (see Figure 4-1):

- Punch cards, in the late 18th century from Herman Hollerith and the Tabulating Machine Company, 1896

- The command-line interface (1960s)

- Sketchpad (1963) by Ivan Sutherland, which was A light pen pointer-based system that created and manipulated objects in drawings

- Alto personal computer (1973), developed at Xerox PARC

- Xerox 8010 Star Information System (1981), which included WIMP/GUI based interactions

- Apple Macintosh (1984)

- Windows 1.01 (1987)

- Microsoft Windows 95

- Mac OSX (2000s)

- Touch devices, such as iOS, Windows 8, and Android

- Voice-based smart assistants on phones, home devices, and speakers

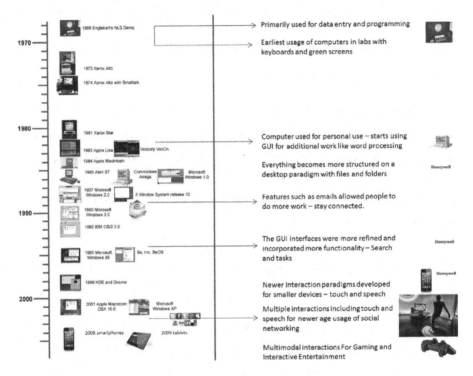

Figure 4-1. *Important evolutions in human computer interactions*

Let's begin by first understanding interactions and interfaces in design.

What Is User Interface Design (UI) and User Experience (UX) Design?

User interface design (UI design) improves interfaces in software or computer devices with a focus on the look or style. The aim of the designer in a UI design is to find an easy-to-use and enjoyable way for users to be able to communicate with the system given a set of tasks that the user wants to perform. To begin understanding how user interfaces are designed, we first need to understand the history of interfaces.

The first mechanical computer was created by Charles Babbage in 1822 and doesn't remotely look like the computers that we work with today. It was considered to be the first automatic computing machine.

IBM introduced its first commercial scientific computer on April 7, 1953, while MIT introduced the core of the basic computer with the first magnetic core RAM and real-time graphics in 1955. Along the way, the size of the computer kept shrinking from using many rooms full of equipment to being able to fit on the user's table as a "desktop".

This computer was limited in its functioning, primarily used only for mathematical purposes. It didn't have a screen, but instead had LEDs, diodes, and all sorts of dials on panels to detect output. These computers were primarily used for research in labs by scientists.

It was only in 1968 that Hewlett-Packard began marketing its HP 9100A as the world's first mass marketed desktop computer. In those machines up until now, the primary way to provide input to the machine was via keyboards and print cards that would allow the computer to understand the inputs.

The Xerox Alto was introduced in 1974 as a revolutionary device, first because it introduced the world to a new way to interact with a computer—using the mouse. It also had a fully functional display screen with windows, menus, and icons as an interface to its operating systems. This was the first form of an interface known in computer devices. It was known as WIMP: Windows, Icons, Menus, and Pointers—and also known as a Graphical User Interface or GUI. This particular version of the interface was dependent on using graphics for allowing the user to interact with the system. Most operating systems, including Windows and Mac OS, operate on this principle today.

In 1979, Steve Jobs visited the Xerox PARC and it was there that he found inspiration in the form of a GUI guided by the mouse. Steve Jobs and Apple launched the Macintosh in 1988 with a simple GUI and mouse, thereby changing how computers were used. Apple quickly sold one million Macintoshes while IBM, Compaq, and others followed with their versions of personal computers around the same time.

Yet another tech company founded by a young computer whiz-kid launched Windows 1.0 in 1985, which would later shape the way future generations would use the computer. Bill Gates dropped out of Harvard to start Microsoft. Windows 3.1 was the bestselling operating system at the time.

Between 1995 and 1997, the laptop computer started overtaking the desktop, and here there were newer ways of interacting with the computer, although incremental. The mouse/keyboard interfaces started becoming much more compact. IBM introduced the track pad on its computer and that quickly started being used instead of the mouse.

Around the same time, a new device called the Palm Pilot was introduced with a new user interface—the stylus, which worked on a touchscreen in the palm of your hand.

In 1997, the Dragon Naturally Speaking Software was launched as the first voice interaction software, but it didn't catch on until much later, in 2010.

In 2000, Apple introduced the first commercially popular optical mouse, following it up later with another mouse with touch and pressure sensitivity. The modern touchpad on the laptop uses these notions. Apple also launched the highly successful iPod music devices with the scroll wheel. The scroll wheel was so successful that Apple actually removed all other physical buttons except the Power button on the device.

In 2007 with the launch of the iPhone, Apple came to the forefront of UI development by creating new paradigms of interacting with the mobile device—using touch to enable users to interact with their phones. Most phones today use touchscreens as the primary method of interacting with the device. The touch didn't just replace the keys of the phone, but unique interactions were also developed, like swiping, pinching to zoom, and rotating the device for implementing natural functions. Google launched its Android OS that most phone manufacturers have since adopted, while those companies that didn't evolve to the new UIs have mostly closed up shop.

While touch became the new way of interacting, since 2011, many companies have developed voice as a user interface as well. Voice assistants like Apple's Siri, Google Now, Amazon Alexa, and Microsoft's Cortana have incorporated voice as a natural method of interaction. The voice-based interfaces have mostly been used in the context of personal assistants, while companies are learning more about the user's behaviors through interpreting the usage data. Today, smart devices such as speakers and assistants have become useful enough to be deployed using only voice to interface with the users.

User Experience Design (UX)

UX design is often confused with UI design, but the key difference between them is that UX design is primarily concerned with how the product functions and how the user experiences the product. User experience is the experience that a person has as they interact with something. One could say that UI is a subset of UX, since the interface allows the user to experience delight. User experience involves understanding the motivations for adopting a product, whether they relate to a task they wish to perform with it, or to values and views associated with the ownership and use of the product.

The term *user experience* was made popular by Donald A. Norman in 1990, as he explained "human interface and usability were too narrow. I wanted to cover all aspects of a person's experience with the system, including industrial design, graphics, the interface and the physical interaction".

User experience design is centered around the entire user journey, i.e. answering what the user can do with a particular use case and then understanding the best way for the user to be able to address that need in a hassle-free and delightful way. One example is the use of a simple animation and accompanying sound that signifies an email being sent from your outbox.

UX design (see Figure 4-2) starts with the why before determining the what and then, finally, the how, in order to create products that users can form meaningful experiences with. In software design, designers must ensure the product's "substance" comes through an existing device and offers a seamless, fluid experience. While designing any interface, the experience of the interface is very important for the user to be able to enjoy the overall interaction.

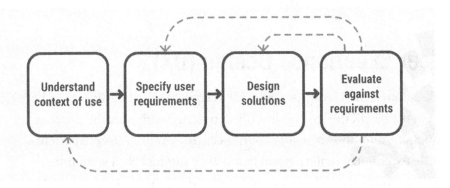

Figure 4-2. *UX design process*

My intention while talking about the interface and experience is not to move away from our original understanding of voice-user interfaces, but to showcase that, while designing such an interface, it is important to understand that your job is to make it easier for the user to complete his task by using all the relevant interaction models available to the user.

Usability and Types of Interactions

Let's not become distracted by the complex talk of devices and interfaces. The original and abiding technical focus of HCI is the concept of usability. Originally conceptualized as "easy to use, easy to learn"—this understanding of HCI gave it an edgy and prominent identity in computing. It held the entire field together and influenced computer science and technology development more broadly and effectively.

Usability in some sense can be identified as trying to make the interactions that have been developed as natural and easy as possible. *Natural* can be identified as the possibility to match or recreate the interactions that humans have in the real world.

Let's look at a few examples:

- One of the biggest design ideas of the 1980s was the introduction of the Macintosh with the desktop paradigm. Files and folders were displayed as icons as an analogy of your desktop. This paradigm has since been renamed "a messy desktop" because of the icons scattered all over the desktop.

  This was definitely an adequate start for the Graphic User interfaces. People can argue that this wasn't the easiest to use or learn, but people grabbed the idea of clicking and dragging windows and icons around their desktop. They also easily lost track of the files and folders that they kept on the desktop, almost as easily as they did on their physical desktops.

- The next shift that happened was from the desktop paradigm to the World Wide Web, or the Internet. Suddenly, the emphasis was on the user interface as it was on the retrieval of information. Email emerged as one of the most important HCI applications, but ironically, email made computers and networks into communication channels. People were not interacting with computers, they were interacting with other people through computers.

- After the web, the next shift in interactions introduced new kinds of devices—laptops, handhelds, etc. The idea of ubiquitous computing emerged from this change in interfaces and can see its applications today in cars, home appliances, furniture, and clothing. The desktop had moved off the desktop.

This allows us to move ahead with the idea introduced a little bit earlier—all interactions are moving toward natural and real-world interactions. Humans spend most of their time trying to communicate with each other or things around them and a foremost mode of communication is through speech. Speech input is quite easy.

Humans perceive the world through their senses and act on it through motor control of their effectors (hands, eyes, legs, and mouth). Computers in a similar way allow users to control it by using input and output mediums like keyboards, mice, tablets, touchscreens, and speakers. The overall goal for most interactions in computers and mobiles is to create an experience that matches the user's real-world interactions as much as possible. For example, flipping a book's page in the real world is replicated by flipping a virtual picture on the smartphone.

There can ideally be two types of interactions that are available for the users:

- Unimodal or a single mode of interaction, in which the user uses only one mode for interacting with the device or the computer.

- Multi-modal interactions, which basically combine two or more unimodal systems to provide more options for the users to interact with the system.

Unimodal systems can be described as a system that is based on a single channel of input, such as touch interactions (WIMP), point and clicks, Graphical User Interfaces (GUI), text-based user interfaces, speech interactions, gestural interactions, and so on. Each of these interactions is used on single channel of input. For example, in a phone, the only way you can provide inputs is by touch interactions (which ideally are an extension of the keyboard and mouse on a computer).

Multi-modal systems are a combination of multiple modalities of interaction by simultaneous use of different input and output channels. The major motivation of the multi-modal system is to provide more natural human interactions.

Unimodal Graphical User Interface Systems (GUI Systems)

This section analyzes the unimodal GUI systems that utilize the WIMP (windows, icons, menus, and pointing devices) system. Traditional WIMP interfaces have the basic premise that information can flow in and out of the system through a single channel or event stream. This event stream can be in the form of input (mouse or keyboard), whereby the user enters data into the system and expects feedback in the form of the output (voice or visual). The input stream can process information one at a time, for example, in today's interaction the computer ignores the typed information (through a keyboard) when a mouse button is pressed.

Compare the WIMP interaction to a multi-modal interaction, whereby the system has multiple event streams and channels and can process information coming through various input modes acting in parallel. For example, users speak while pointing to a piece of information on the screen.

Traditional WIMP interfaces reside on a single machine; multi-modal systems are spread across multiple networks and systems that all perform their specific actions—like speech processing and gesture recognition.

Graphical User Interfaces (GUI)/WIMP Interactions

These were the first type of GUIs and were based on the WIMP system. These were created with the end user in mind, which were not necessarily scientists and mathematicians.

As the computer became more and more personal, companies tried enticing consumers to start using computers in their everyday lives. GUIs were created to make the computer more user-friendly and they used graphics instead of the traditional command-line interfaces.

The computer desktop was touted as the only thing you would need on your office desktop as a productivity tool. The Apple Macintosh, Windows OS, and Xerox PARC made this user interface popular, and computers primarily used this interface style for decades.

Voice Interactions

Speech interactions have lately had a big impact especially given the success of Apple's personal assistant Siri. People have been exposed to an assistant that they think can truly understand what they ask for—and the truth is that Siri is not only a voice recognition client but also has built-in semantics, which means it tries to make "meaning" from your queries.

Speech interactions (see Figure 4-3) are the most natural form of interaction that we have, whether with other humans or computers. It's easiest for a human to give instructions or queries verbally. The user satisfaction is highly dependent on the user's tasks and profiles. The learning curve for speech interaction is low.

Figure 4-3. *Google speech*

But speech interactions offer certain difficulties—especially around social usage constraints. Users cannot use speech in certain public spaces, since doing so would invade the user's privacy (imagine that you want to log in to your bank account but you need to say the password out loud on a bus to do so).

The technology that implements speech recognition isn't completely accurate yet, and it still creates errors, which is a big concern in its implementation.

Gestural Interfaces

Gestural interactions have been around for some time, but were made extremely famous and well known courtesy of devices like Microsoft Kinect (see Figure 4-4) and Leap Motion (see Figure 4-5). Hackers and technologists soon started using the Kinect and Leap Motion for a lot more than just gaming and gestural interfaces. A gesture is a motion of the body that contains information. Waving goodbye is a gesture, but pressing a key on a keyboard is not a gesture since the motion of pressing a key is not important for an action. The important part is which key was pressed.

Gestures (Billing Hurst, 2011) though interesting vary in their application. This also means that each gesture can mean a different thing in each application. Gestural interaction is mapped to specific tasks and hence is limited in application—since there are limited universal gestures.

Gestural interactions are mostly based on habits developed from mouse usage (like the zooming in function of a mouse—enabling spreading of fingers or hands to zoom in on a gestural interface).

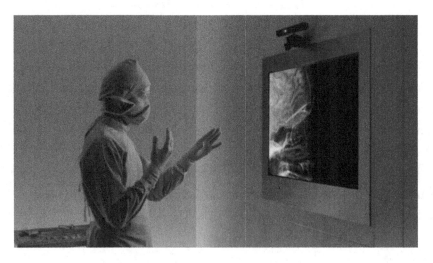

Figure 4-4. *Hospital Kinect usage*

The main advantage of a gestural interaction is that it is direct and reliable. But gestural interactions are limited by spatial constraints and cannot be used in places where the body cannot be identified or tracked. Smaller sensors like the Leap Motion technology still require a certain distance away from the sensor to track the hand gestures of the users. Also, gestural interaction cannot be used in a socially active surrounding and require a certain degree of privacy or isolation to be effectively deployed.

Figure 4-5. *Leap Motion*

Haptics

The word "haptics" is derived from the Greek word haptestahi, which means to touch. Manipulation tasks in the real world require feeling objects and dynamics. This basically can be explained as the means through which the devices give back a feeling of sensation to the user; for example, vibratory feedback.

Haptic or force feedback interfaces are interfaces where a small robot applies a computer-controlled forces to the user's hand. It represents a virtual environment and acts both as an input and output device. Users feel and control at the same time. Let's look at a small example of the most widely used haptic feedback device. The airplane cockpit control wheel is a valid example that gives haptic feedback to the pilot when the pilot moves the plane more than the set limit.

Haptic interfaces are often multi-modal and rely on many senses to detect and give output, such as sight and sound. The potential benefits of using haptic feedback are involve comfort and aesthetics:

- Pleasant tactility

- Satisfying motion and dynamics

- Ergonomics

- Muscle memory

- Personalization affect and communication affect and communication

- Social context and presence to mediated user-user or user-machine connections

Multi-Modal Interactions

Multi-modal interactions (MMIs) are a way to make user interfaces natural and efficient with parallel and meaningful use of two or more input or output modalities. Multi-modal systems can combine two or more user input modes, such as speech, pen, touch, manual gestures, gaze, and head/body movements in a coordinated manner.

Most interactions on virtual devices were created similar to the interactions that humans have in the real physical world. This is because the aim of any interaction on an interface is to make the interaction as natural as possible. Consider the case of the Amazon Kindle. The way a user turns the page by swiping down on the right-top corner of an actual book is replicated on the device. This along with the feature of creating a paler background color than a pure white on the kindle device allows users to experience the Kindle device as similar to the experience of reading a physical book.

Needless to say, that the Kindle cannot replace the experience of reading the book—that's the difference of the medium itself—but it can allow the user to use a familiar method of interacting with the device while using past knowledge about how the users read an actual book.

Some examples of multi-modal interactions are shown in Figures 4-6 through 4-8.

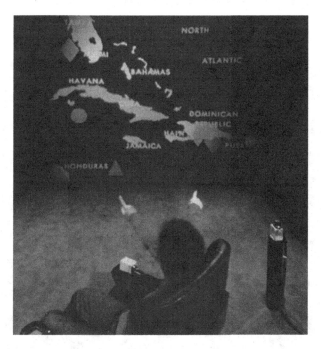

Figure 4-6. *Example of a multi-modal interaction*

Figure 4-7. *Microsoft Xbox Kinect*

Figure 4-8. *Demo of Google Glass*

The ultimate goal of all interface systems is to make sure that the user can complete the goal/task without realizing that she is using an interface to do it.

In the real world, humans seldom perform tasks using a unimodal approach. Let's look at an example of a multi-modal interaction using voice. We will work with our assistant Max for this example.

> *Me: Hey Max, what movies are playing in the theatre near me?*
>
> *Max: A quick search shows that Movie A, Movie B, and Movie C are playing in Location A, which is closest to you. Would you like me to book a seat for you?*
>
> *User: Nice, can you tell me the showings for Movie A?*
>
> *Max: Sure, Movie A is playing at location A with shows available at 12pm, 1:30pm, 5pm, and 8:30pm.*
>
> *User: Can you book the show at 5pm for me?*
>
> *Max: Sure, I have sent the details of the show on your phone. You can use BookMyMovie app to book the show.*
>
> *Max: Have fun at the movies. I'll set a reminder once you have completed the booking on your device.*

Now, as you can imagine, determining which movies are playing near you is easy enough to do using a VUI interface, but the next steps require the user to finish the booking on his mobile device. This is because it wouldn't be natural to visualize which seat numbers you would want. All theatres have different seat arrangements, so you need to see which seats you want. Secondly, today's voice systems are not secure enough to use for payment purposes. Would you be comfortable speaking your card numbers out in public for anyone to be able to hear and use?

This is a great use case for a multi-modal interaction, since you start the task of booking a movie using the voice interface, but switch to your mobile device screen to complete the task, in order to select seats and make payments.

Multi-modal interactions can be classified as the following:

- **Perceptual interactive**—They are highly interactive, rich, natural, and effective

- **Attentive**—They are context-aware and implicit

- **Enactive**—They communicate information that relies on active manipulation through the use of hands or body

Unimodal Graphical User Interface Systems (GUI Systems) vs Multi-Modal Interfaces

Let's start by discussing the advantages of multi-modal systems over unimodal systems.

There are certain advantages (ali[1]) that a multi-modal system has over a unimodal system:

1. They are more natural. Naturalness follows from the free choice of modalities and may result in a human computer interaction that is closer to human-human interaction.

    a. Different modalities excel at different tasks.

    b. They are more engaging to the users because users can do multiple things at once (speak and use hand gestures or gaze to select an option).

---

[1]Gabriel skantze (KTH Royal Institute of Technology, Sweden)

2. Improved error handling and efficiency allows for fewer errors and faster task completion. Imagine when using a login form in which you have to enter an email address. You would have seen that there is always a default text written for the user to understand what they need to type (see Figure 4-9).

| X Don't | ✓ Do |

Figure 4-9. *Default text helps readers know what to type*

3. Greater precision in visual and spatial tasks (such as map scrolling and item localization on map).

4. Support for the user's preferred interaction style. For example, if we were to navigate the UI shown in Figure 4-10, we could simply use voice to search for particular content or use the keyboard to navigate through the list. Both interaction styles are available.

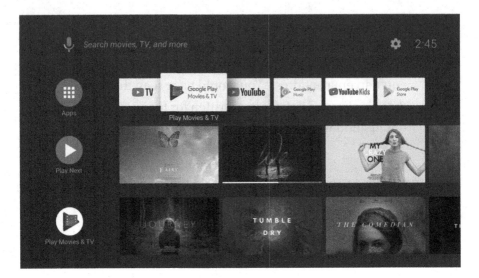

Figure 4-10. *Multiple modes of interaction are available*

5. Accommodation of diverse users, tasks, and usage
    environments. A simple example of this point is how
    users on any phone device can change the size of
    the icons and text for the UI. See Figure 4-11.

smaller point size.

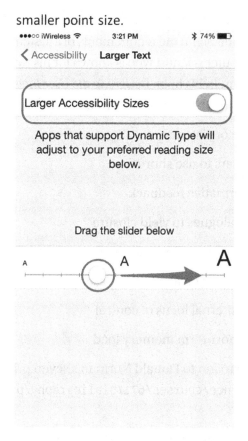

Figure 4-11. Interaction can accommodate different user needs

Principles of User Interactions

Multi-modal interfaces need to be created with different contexts in which a solution will be used, while understanding the needs and abilities of the different types of users who will interact with the system. This dynamic adaptation enables the interface to utilize various modes of input that complement each other so that users can perform the task they need to complete.

For most things, there are a set of guidelines and principles that are used as benchmarks to understand the requirements of a system. Ben Shneiderman is an American computer scientist who is known for his work in human computer interactions. In his book *Designing the User Interface: Strategies for Effective HCI,* he explains his eight golden rules for interface design:

- Strive for consistency

- Enable users to use shortcuts

- Offer informative feedback

- Design dialogues to yield closure

- Offer error prevention and simple error handling

- Permit easy reversal of actions

- Support internal locus of control

- Reduce short-term memory load

This is in comparison to Donald Norman's seven principles (http://www.csun.edu/science/courses/671/bibliography/preece.html), as follows:

- Use both knowledge of the real world and knowledge in the head

- Simplify the structure of the tasks

- Make things visible; bridge the gap between execution and evaluation

- Get the mapping right

- Exploit the power of constraint, both natural and artificial

- Design for error

- When all else fails, standardize

But the most widely used principles are Nielsen's heuristics (Nielsen, 1995, `https://www.nngroup.com/articles/ten-usability-heuristics/`):

- Visibility of system status

- Match the system and the real world

- User control and freedom

- Consistency and standards

- Flexibility and efficiency

- Error prevention

- Error reporting, diagnosis, and recovery

- Aesthetic and minimalist design

- Recognition rather than recall

- Help and documentation

The guiding principles mentioned here are strategies that allow you as the designer to figure out a strategy for your interfaces. These help you understand the optimal method for implementing your interfaces, regardless of whether it's a unimodal interaction or multi-modal interaction. You can determine the most intuitive and effective combinations for the required application.

The next section explains Nielsen's heuristics in more detail and illustrates exactly what each of these points mean.

Visibility of System Status

Provide the user with timely and appropriate feedback about the system's current status.

Natural and Intuitive: Match the Real World

This heuristic basically refers to the idea of speaking the user's language using terms and concepts that are familiar to the intended audience. Information should be organized naturally and logically based on the what users are accustomed to seeing in the real world.

Control of the Interaction Should Lie with the User

Humans are most comfortable when they feel in control of themselves and their environment. Thoughtless software and devices take away from that comfort by forcing people into unplanned interactions, confusing paths (menus and submenus), and unexpected outcomes. We should keep the users in control by regularly reporting about system status, by describing causation (for example, if you do this then that will happen), and by giving insights into what will happen next.

Flexibility of System Status

We should be able to anticipate the user's needs and wants whenever possible. Novice and expert users interact with the system differently. The system should be easy and efficient to use by novices and experts alike. This means providing "accelerators" for expert users to more efficiently navigate your application to complete common tasks. For example, pressing Alt+Tab to switch an app or Ctrl+Q to quit.

Match the User's Mental Model and Reduce Cognitive Load (also by Consistency)

Reduce the memory load of users by presenting familiar icons, actions, and options whenever possible. Do not require the user to recall information from one screen to another.

Error Recovery: User's Commands and Actions Can Be Reversed

Even better than good error messages is a careful design that prevents a problem from occurring in the first place. Either eliminate error-prone conditions or check for them and present users with a confirmation option before they commit the action.

Aesthetic and Minimalist Design

A minimalist design is a design stripped down to only its essential elements. Only the essential parts are left, nothing more. Needless things have been omitted.

Now that we have read the various guidelines, what does it all mean?

During the past decade we have witnessed a complete change in how users access information and store knowledge, especially with the technological advances of the mobile phones that are more than capable of performing complex tasks and a variety of functions. Another benefit that has happened is the access to high-speed and affordable Internet access across the world. These advances have presented opportunities for natural interactions, moving beyond the touchscreens to voice and gestural based interactions as well.

We are now seeing an ecosystem of inter-connected devices, whether it is our smartphones, smart TVs, smart speakers, smart cars, or smart homes. We, as designers, will need to provide novel approaches for interacting with all this digital content across all these devices in a natural way. Obviously, we cannot explore the complete range of interfaces and interaction across all devices for the purpose of this book; hence, we will limit our scope to discussing the multi-modal interactions with respect to voice-user interfaces.

Voice Interactions vs Multi-Modal Interactions

Today communication through speech and language is one of the most challenging modalities for machines. While undoubtedly, this kind of interaction is the most natural, it requires high bandwidth, data processing capabilities, and a complete two-way communication channel.

Companies like Google, Microsoft, Amazon, and Apple have invested heavily into developing natural language processing capabilities, machine learning, and artificial intelligence to implement speech as a form of natural interaction.

Simple commands and tasks, such as making a phone call, setting a reminder, and speech to text are easy to do using today's speech user interfaces, but the moment we try to create use cases regarding the user's intent and try to understand the meaning behind what the user is saying, most of these systems are still lacking.

It becomes imperative for the voice-based interface system to be able to allow interactions through multiple modes and perform the tasks that the user wants to complete.

Natural interactions of speech or gesture are often considered error-prone and most systems are designed with alternate interactions in place. Speech interaction in particular requires a hands-free and eyes-free interaction.

Obviously, with all the languages, dialects, and intentions in the world, these systems will always be prone to error, but that does not mean that these systems cannot be useful. All it takes is a proper interaction design that can complement speech interactions.

As with a regular human conversation, you might not always receive the information that you are looking for, but more often than not, the conversations are mostly helpful in finding the right solutions.

In today's world of helpful digital assistants, most users often have limited interactions with them—such as asking about the weather, asking basic trivia questions, helping set a reminder, or playing a particular soundtrack a streaming service. This is usually perceived as a mismatch between the "affordance" or, simply put, the actionable properties between the interaction of speech and the user, and the ability of the speech as a method of interaction.

Emerging Multi-Modal Principles

Different multi-modal interactions excel at different tasks.

- There is no one way to apply multi-modal interactions since by definition multi-modal interactions use two or more modalities for either input or output.

  For example, speech is convenient for data entry but since its feedback for data input is long and verbose, it can lead to bad error recovery situations.

  Touch is a more preferred way to perform data input, since it allows instant error recovery and the feedback is visual in nature for the user to observe, correct, and review.

- For an action-based command, a user might prefer speech since it is more direct and relates to how humans in everyday life give commands.

  For example, lock the door or turn off the kitchen lights.

  For example, in touch/GUI it will take a click of a button, but to come to the same action it will take a greater number of clicks to reach the automation to turn on the lights.

95

- Touch systems (GUI systems) are better at giving information back to the user. The user can visually observe the status and errors all at once on the screen. While speech takes a longer time to do the same to speak the same status. Also, speech uses a single modality to give back information (auditory), but we as humans can observe a lot better via gaze (sight) than hear a lot of information.

- Each user can have her preferences of modality and hence the idea is to allow usage of multi-modal interaction but let the users decide which ones they are comfortable with.

  The situational awareness is also required to use the right modality at the right place.

  For example, for privacy concerns no one would like to use speech interactions in a busy control room, or a place where people could easily understand what you are up to, but speech can be used perfectly when no one is monitoring your interactions. Social concerns are also important to understand which modality to use.

Designing the Voice-Based Interface

As discussed previously, the best interfaces are the ones that appear to be invisible to the end user or the most natural. In this aspect, voice interfaces can be easily considered much more natural since the user appears to interact with the voice-user interface as comfortably as they would with another human being.

To design an interface, we need to understand what the interface is going to be used for. In this context, let's look again at trying to create an interface to book a movie ticket using voice.

Now we are assuming that our solution has to utilize voice, hence our solution will be to create a voice-user interface in addition to any other additional modes that we use.

Before we start, let's figure out whom our end users are. If we were to assume that our voice solution is to be used in a voice-based user interaction in a smart home speaker, where the home would consist of kids and their parents, then that would be a good start. Now let's look at Nielsen's principles for designing an interface.

Match the system and the real world. This means that we have to realize how movie tickets are booked in the real world. Let's try to decipher this step by step:

1. A user has to realize that he wants to watch a movie. (Intent)

2. A user tries to find the listing of the latest movies that he/she can watch. (Information Gathering)

3. A user tries to find the places the movie that he/she wants to watch is available. Ideally this place should be nearby.

4. A user decides how many tickets how many tickets for the show he wants.

5. A user approaches the place where he wants to watch the movie.

6. The user walks up to the information desk to find out which movie shows and seats are available for the latest show. This would be through a conversation with the movie ticket booking clerk.

7.   The user would ideally select the seats of choice and then pay for the tickets. (Action)

8.   The user would then get a printout of his tickets that he can show while entering the movie theater. (Goal Completed)

Now, most of this looks trivial, right? Who goes to the movie theater to book a ticket; we just go there to watch the movie. Today, with the ease of use of mobile apps and web sites combined with an always connected Internet, users simply log on to the web site of their choice and book their shows with a few simple clicks.

You would agree though all these steps are followed to book the tickets, while the conversation with the movie ticket booking clerk is the only step that is replaced by simply showing the user the available movie show timings and seat availability.

If that is the case, why do we even need to create a new interface in voice? Well here's where it gets interesting. To do the entire process, you need to have a screen (mobile or laptop). What if you don't? What if you were only able to use your voice (see Figure 4-12)?

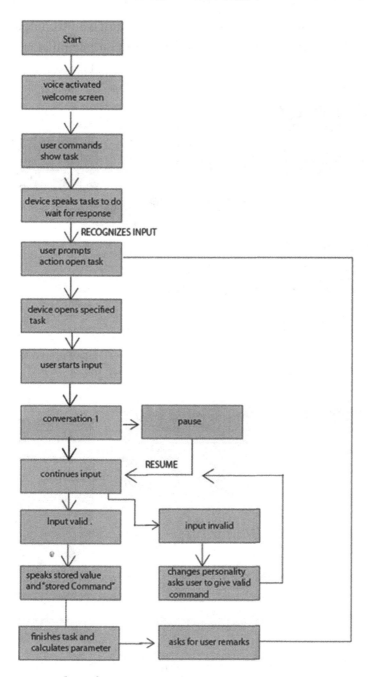

Figure 4-12. *What if you were only able to use your voice to buy a movie ticket*

Let's try to understand how our speech assistant would compare to booking a movie ticket versus a different mode of interaction. Let's try using our smartphone without the assistant first; see Figure 4-13.

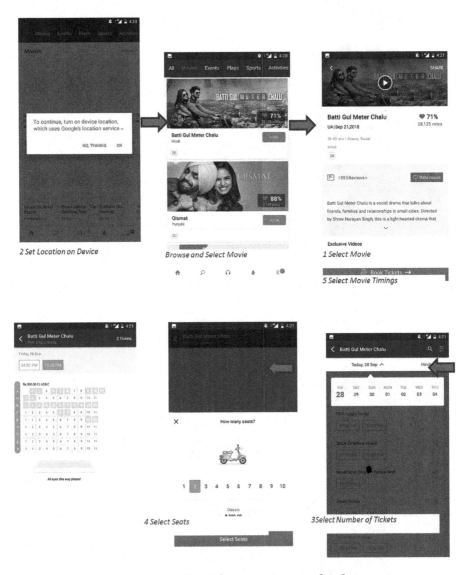

Figure 4-13. *Buying a movie ticket requires multiple steps*

Now let's try simple voice commands to book a ticket, as shown in Figure 4-14.

6 Make Payment and Confirmation

9 Asking the Assistant for the latest Movies Near Me

7 Review Booking Summary

8 We get a listing of Movies on the Screen as search Results

Figure 4-14. *Using voice commands to buy a movie ticket*

As you can see, simply booking a movie ticket using speech interaction is currently difficult. The assistant was able to essentially help us from an accessibility point of view, but eventually just gave us a listing of the movies as a search result.

What if we had to go through the entire process of booking the ticket using voice?

Well, we would need many features set up for it to work properly, including setting the right locations and understanding that the listing should display results on the basis of the location nearest to me. The assistant can only help assist our entire task, not do it completely for us in today's scenario, since for the final step of making a payment it would be currently difficult to use payments via using voice. They aren't allowed currently (due to legal and security implications).

Figure 4-15 compares the interactions with the earlier principles to understand which points are missing in booking a movie ticket using both interactions.

Interactions	Natural and Intuitive	Visibility of System Status	Control	Flexibility & Efficiency	Match User Mental Modal	Error Recovery	Aesthetic & Minimal design
Touch Current Interaction	✓	✓	✓	✓	✓	✓	✓
Remarks	Touch Interactions offer a tangible interface for user's interaction For e.g: something similar to actual on/off switches.	While Booking the movie tickets using the smartphone, we can check out every stage of the process step by step clearly.	The user has complete control from finding the listing of the movies , to the availability of the tickets, to being able to finally book the ticket The user still requires to go through multiple	Touch interactions don't allow easy navigation to shortcuts for arming and disarming functions. For eg. A user can store the location where he / she would watch the movies by default , apart from storing payment details for	The GUI matches the users mental mode of how to go ahead and book a movie ticket. Exploring the movie timings and booking details as understood by the user.	In case you are about to book the ticket , there are multiple screens for review of the booking summary before the payment are made.	GUI design can be said to conform to a minimalistic design and adhere with UI guidelines on the screen.
Speech Current Interaction	✓	✗	✗	✗	✗	✗	✓
	The ability to explore new movies playing are easy to use , while asking about the locations near by where the timings are available are quite normal.	This visibility of the system status with respect to only a smart speaker based system is limited only to the device understanding the query or not. Nothing more which makes it difficult for a user to comprehend the current state of the system.	The user has to wait for the conversation with the system to understand whether he/ she has to redo the action or not. The use is never in complete control of the system	Speech Interaction allows clear conversations , but the moment an action has to be completed the efficiency is dependent on how clearly the system understands the users intent.	Speech should be used in the form that humans speak it , but sometime some actions are unable to be completed using Speech , for eg: choosing seats or making payments in the current form.	The error recovery of the system is limited to the current context of the conversation with the system, or we have to start from the begining.	The only design required here is the right voice interface to interact with the user to give and accept information's.

Figure 4-15. *Comparing speech and touch interactions*

Summary

As you can see, multi-modal interactions are quite useful whenever the system is unable to fulfill the particular task desired by the user in the simplest or most meaningful way.

You can never decide to use only a single modality from the start, but instead designers have to understand the requirement of the users to complete a particular task based on the system's input and output modalities.

Interfaces are designed by understanding the user's needs to help solve a particular task. As discussed, there are several use cases for which a unimodal system is useful, but there are cases where unimodal systems alone cannot complete the task without adding interfaces.

In this chapter, we discussed that there are several guidelines that we can refer to, including Shneiderman's and Norman's principles, that allow us to design an interface for an task. These guidelines allow users to create a checklist before choosing the best interface for the job. Certain constraints and inflexibilities will call for choosing one interaction over another, and it becomes important to create a responsible, user-friendly design interaction that the users feel is naturally comfortable to use.

Index

A, B

Alexa, 3–4, 8, 10
Anthropomorphism, 26, 39
Apple, 72
Automated Speech Recognition
       (ASR), 2

C

Chatbots, 4–5
Cognitive engineering, 69
Conversation
       machine, 55
Conversations, 14
   casual, 27
   criteria, 14
   design, 14
   intent-based, 27
Cortana, 1

D, E, F

Designing the User Interface:
    Strategies for Effective
    HCI, 90
Digital assistants,
      chatbots, 4–5
Duplex model, 55

G

Gestural interactions, 80–81
Gimmicky interactions, 94
Google, 1, 8
Google Assistant/Allo, 8, 30
Google Home, 8
Google Now, 8
Google speech, 79
Graphical User Interface Systems
      (GUI Systems), 72
   unimodal, 77–78
   WIMP interactions, 78

H

Haptics, 81–82
Hesitation markers, 55
Human-computer interaction
      (HCI), 68–69
   cognitive engineering, 69
   developments, 69
   evolutions, 69–70

I, J, K

Interactions
   examples, 75–76
   gestural, 80–81

Interactions (*cont.*)
  multi-modal, 77
  unimodal, 77
  voice, 78–79
Interactive voice response (IVR)
  systems, 1, 3

L

Leap Motion technology, 81

M

Mirror neurons, 40
Multi-modal interactions
    (MMIs), 67, 77, 82
  Amazon Kindle, 82
  classifications, 86
  example, 83, 85
  Google glass, demo, 84
  Microsoft Xbox Kinect, 84
  principles, 95–96
  unimodal GUI systems *vs.*,
    86–89

N, O

Natural Language Understanding
    (NLU), 2

P, Q, R

Palm Pilot, 72
Personality

adding pauses, 56
  agreeableness, 57
  conscientiousness, 57
  Cortana, 63–64
  extraversion, 57
  Google assistant, 61–62
  Max, 59–60, 65
  mirroring, 59
  neuroticism, 57
  openness to experience, 57
  opinions and preferences, 61
  preferences and
    interests, 65
  single turn *vs.* multi-turn
    conversations, 58
  tech limitation, 58
  user's emotions, 64
  creating, 42–43
  hesitation markers, 55
  voice assistant (*see* Voice
    assistant)
*Plans and Situated Actions: The
    Problem of Human-Machine
    Communication*, 21
Principles
  cooperate and
    respond, 26–28, 30–31
  leverage context, 21
    analysis, 23–24
    conversational context, 25
    emotional context, 25–26
    example, 22–24
    physical context, 25
  progressive disclosure, 31, 33

recognize intent
    analysis, 18, 20
    example, 16–19
    GUI, 16
    high-utility interaction, 15
    low-utility interaction, 15
  turn-taking, 35
  variety, 34–35
Progressive disclosure, 31, 33

S, T
Shoebox, 2
Siri, 3–4, 8

U
Unimodal interactions, 77
  GUI systems, 77–78
  vs. MMIs, 86–89
User experience, 74
User experience design
  (UX design), 73–74
User interactions
  principles, 90–91
  rules, 90
  system status, flexibility
    aesthetic and minimalist
      design, 93
    error recovery, 93
    memory load of users, 92
  system status, visibility
    control, 92
    natural and intuitive, 92

voice interactions *vs.*
  MMIs, 94–95
User interface design
  (UI design), 71–73

V
Verge, 9
Voder, 2
Voice assistant
  building networks, 52
  Cortana, 44, 46–47
  deep neural networks, 50
  Duplex model, 55
  Google Assistant, 46
  Google Duplex, 50–51
  handling real-world tasks, 51
  interacting with virtual
    entity, 47
  interactive experience, 44
  interconnections, 53–54
  killer VUI, 44
  Max, 51, 53
  microexpressions, 49
  Microsoft or Amazon, 43
  Ruuh chatbot avatar, 45
  Sophia (humanoid robot), 48
Voice interaction, 67
  designing
    movie ticket
      booking, 98, 100–102
    speech and touch
      interactions, 102
    steps, 97–98

Voice interaction (*cont.*)
  hands free, 6
  intuitive, 6
  linguistic alignment, 7
  personas, 7
  speed, 6
Voice user interface (VUI), 1
  explosion, 1
  landscape, 8–10

W

Windows, Icons, Menus,
  and Pointers
  (WIMP), 72

X, Y, Z

Xerox Alto, 71
Xerox PARC, 72

Printed in the United States
By Bookmasters